A
From Weary to Wholehearted

"Between global pandemic, racial trauma, church decline, personal loss, and social turmoil, it's okay to admit we are *not* okay. Callie Swanlund gives voice to our collective weariness, even as she speaks powerful words of wisdom, courage, healing, and hope to clergy, lay leaders, and caring professionals everywhere. Even if you don't identify as 'burned out,' the reflections and practices in *From Weary to Wholehearted* will feel like fresh rainwater poured on parched land. Read this book—it will restore your spark."

—Stephanie Spellers, Canon to the Presiding Bishop for
Evangelism, Reconciliation, and Creation Care; author of
*Radical Welcome: Embracing God, the Other, and the Spirit of
Transformation* and *The Church Cracked Open: Disruption,
Decline, and New Hope for Beloved Community*

"If you're a hardworking pastor or a passionate justice advocate in the church or elsewhere in these stressful times, this book may save your life! Callie Swanlund offers a splendid resource for all caregivers and social activists who care deeply about their own physical, mental, and spiritual health as well as their strong, ongoing commitments to others. The book, which includes important reflection questions and a multitude of real-life stories, is beautifully written and designed to be used as an ongoing resource."

—Carter Heyward, professor emerita of
the Episcopal Divinity School and author of
*The Seven Deadly Sins of White Christian
Nationalism: A Call to Action*

"If you have been feeling worried, wearied, or worn in ministry, this book is for you. *From Weary to Wholehearted* is a much-needed spark for church leaders seeking to reignite their passion for following Jesus along the way. Callie offers a deeply pastoral and truly refreshing companion guide to help Church leaders rediscover the immense passion at the heart of our call."

—Deon K. Johnson, Bishop,
the Episcopal Diocese of Missouri

"In a time when pandemic, violence, changes in church and community can leave us in a state of near burnout, heartbreak, weariness of soma and soul, Callie Swanlund's beautiful book is a lifegiving spark. Through liturgical season and personal story, it offers a memorable, practical, and transformative model that can function as an invitational flint to ignite wholeheartedness in ministry, not just for weary clergy and aspiring seminarians but for all who are enflamed by the Holy."

—Storm Swain, the Frederick Houk Borsch
Associate Professor of Anglican Studies, Pastoral Care,
and Theology at United Lutheran Seminary

"What I appreciated the most about *From Weary to Wholehearted* was how it addressed the moments in life where we feel unsettled, where we are neither fully alive nor dead. Callie acknowledges the difficulty of these moments, but also highlights the importance of sitting with our emotions, searching our souls, and waiting with our hearts. Throughout the book, she reminds us that God is with us, whether we are in moments of joy or grief. I highly recommend *From Weary to Wholehearted* to anyone who is looking for guidance on how to navigate vulnerability, grief, and the in-between moments of life. Callie's insights are transformative and will leave you feeling empowered, hopeful, and, yes, wholehearted."

—Roger Hutchison, author of *The Art of Calm: Spiritual Exercises for the Anxious Soul*

"Callie Swanlund is the real deal, and this book is an absolute treasure for those who are weary and heavy-laden. With grace, compassion, and practical wisdom, *From Weary to Wholehearted* is an oasis in the desert of clergy burnout. For all of my clergy siblings who are suffering in these anxious times, find the courage to open this book and let the Holy Spirit speak to you through this resource. You won't be disappointed. Thank you, Callie, for this remarkable guide. It is a gift to the Church. I will recommend it to clergy everywhere."

—Traci Smith, leadership coach and author of the Faithful Families series

"In this new era of ministry, emerging after a global pandemic, we need Rev. Callie Swanlund's love letter to lay leaders and clergy. She understands the weariness that leaders are feeling. She responds with generous and inspiring remedies for healing the whole heart, body, mind, and spirit. Each SPARK Practice calls us to remember who we are deep in our bones, to make our thoughtful plans, to lean into wonder, to rest often, and to know we are not alone."

—Eileen Campbell-Reed, author of *Pastoral Imagination: Bringing the Practice of Ministry to Life*, visiting associate professor of pastoral theology and care at Union Theological Seminary, codirector of the Learning Pastoral Imagination Project, founder and host of *Three Minute Ministry Mentor*

From Weary
to Wholehearted

From Weary to Wholehearted

A RESTORATIVE RESOURCE FOR OVERCOMING CLERGY BURNOUT

CALLIE E. SWANLUND

Church Publishing
19 East 34th Street
New York, NY 10016
www.churchpublishing.org

Cover by Callie E. Swanlund
Typeset by Nord Compo

A record of this book is available from the Library of Congress.

ISBN 978-1-64065-678-9 (pbk)
ISBN 978-1-64065-679-6 (ebook)

For E,
whose courage makes me strive for a more loving world

For L,
who always draws me back to joy

For J,
who sees my spark and asks how it can shine brighter

The Wayfarer's Index

A Welcome
to Weary Travelers

Welcome, dear ones. Whether you're ordained clergy, a lay ministry professional, or someone who has experienced or witnessed burnout in another vocation, I'm so glad you're here.

I want to speak this truth from the very beginning: people in outward-facing professions are weary. Within the world of the Church, our recent shared history has brought about collegial loneliness, ever-changing ministry practices, abundant illness and death, and declining church attendance. As an Episcopal priest, ministry coach, and retreat leader, I have witnessed firsthand the impact all of this has had on faith leaders.

Many of us report finding less joy in our ministry, are contemplating a radical vocational change, or have already left traditional ministry altogether. Our mental health is also precarious. Anecdotally, I know of a large handful of priests and lay leaders who have recently died by suicide or entered inpatient treatment for mental health. There is a crisis at hand.

From Weary to Wholehearted isn't a quick fix but a companion to remind faith leaders you're not alone, to give you sustainable tools for finding joy and rest, and to reground you in spiritual nourishment. In this book, I invite you to show up with your whole heart, vulnerably and courageously. We will address sources of weariness, like loneliness, overwhelm, comparison to others, lack of inspiration, and more. I have incorporated research in the fields of sociology and psychology, as well as my personal experience as a faith leader and a companion to other faith leaders. You'll be guided by scripture, personal meditation, reflection prompts, prayer, and a SPARK Practice for flourishing.

My dear friend Heidi and I began offering digital Advent and Lenten quiet days for clergy women during the pandemic, and we described our offerings as love letters to our sibling clergy. This book is indeed a love letter to all who are weary.

Do you want to be made well?

In John 5, Jesus encounters a man who has been ill for thirty-eight years. He asks the man, "Do you want to be made well?" I ask you the same. It's easy to point to reasons why your flourishing is on hold, the many external forces in your way. Those things are real. As the man in John says, "I have no one to put me into the pool when the water is stirred up, and while I am making my way someone else steps down ahead of me."

And yet, we must also claim our own healing. We must also *desire* our own healing. We must want to be made well. So I ask you, dear ones, do you want to be made well?

There are some truths I'll return to again and again—my three sermons, if you will. I ask that you trust me on these:

You are beloved.
You have a light that the world so deeply needs.
You are not alone.

If this book transforms you, that's wonderful, but I want you to know that you are already enough, *right now, as you are.*

An Invitation Toward Flourishing: SPARK Practice

Not long ago, my family spent an inordinate amount of hours and dollars on our physical and mental health. In one calendar year, I had my gall bladder removed out of concern for a potentially cancerous polyp, went on anti-anxiety meds (see organ removal and medical bills), spent several months in a boot for a broken toe, dealt with kidney stones and subsequent infections, and supported loved ones through their own mental and physical woes. As the year came to a close, I began to exhale a sigh of relief, thinking our bad fortune was nearly behind us. That is, until I woke up on December 28 with shingles wrapping around my torso.

I knew something needed to give. I chose the chain of words *tend/tender/tended* to anchor my life through the next season. Tend, for the ways in which I needed to tend to my own healing in body and soul. Tender, for the ways in which I needed to let the tenderness of my heart lead rather than donning an elusive armor of strength. Tended, for the ways in which I needed to entrust others with a share in my care, rather than always attempting to go it alone.

I'm almost embarrassed to admit how much this shift healed me, because I don't want to feed into the culture of magical manifestation—the idea that we can bring about something good simply by speaking it out loud. But what I began to experience was not something that centered self to the exclusion of God and my neighbor. It was a fullness of life rooted in the Holy, with deep nurture of myself and my connection with others.

Though there are many external factors that can profoundly impact your sense of overwhelm, you are invited to be participants in your own flourishing. At the heart of this book is a *SPARK Practice*, a holistic wellness method for finding flourishing in mind, body, and spirit. The SPARK Practice I introduce below is intended as just that—a spark. It is a fire starter, a catalyst toward the fullness of life into which God beckons each of us.

I created this practice from both my own experience as someone living in languishing and my years of companionship with countless ministry leaders, and by drawing on the scholarship of many wisdom bearers: primarily sociologist Brené Brown, in whose research on vulnerability, shame, trust, and empathy I'm trained; as well as burnout experts Emily and Amelia Nagoski; psychologist Martin Seligman; Indigenous author Kaitlin Curtice; and Indigenous botanist Robin Wall Kimmerer.

At the end of each section of this book, I invite you into your own SPARK Practice, centered around these five elements and described in greater detail below:

nurture my **S**oma
engage in **P**reparation
make space for **A**we
claim **R**etreat
ground myself in **K**inship

There is no correct way to engage in this practice. There isn't a prescribed order, but rather interwoven elements that I encourage you to make space for in your daily or weekly lives. Each section's SPARK Practice will give tips and exercises that pertain to that particular source of weariness, so you may find it helpful to return to that part when you experience it. Over time, you might move to a weekly examen model—the Ignatian spiritual exercise of reflecting on God's presence in your life—that incorporates these five elements: soma, preparation, awe, retreat, and kinship.

It may work best for you to choose one specific element to focus on for an entire season, especially if it's one that jumps off the page to you or makes you the most uncomfortable. What you need most might be the thing you most long for *or* the thing you meet with the greatest resistance.

You will notice a natural flow to the practice: body, mind, spirit, time set apart, and time focused on others. Awe, of course, is at the very center, a compass when you feel lost. This tool provides a way to re-orient your life toward flourishing and anchor yourself in the things that are most life-giving.

Nurture My Soma

The S stands for Soma, which is Greek for *body*. The word "soma" is found more than 140 times in Christian scripture to refer to human bodies. It's also used to refer to the celestial bodies of the sun, moon, and stars—a reminder that we are deeply intertwined with the universe God created.

When we find ourselves in burnout, the best ways to move beyond stress are all somatic. Researchers found that movement is the number one way to complete the stress cycle, but other ways we can respond bodily are through breath, physical touch, laughter, and tears.

When I write about Soma, I'm talking about the ways in which you *view* your body, the ways in which you *nourish* your body, and the ways in which you *check in* with your body. Though we sometimes forget to tend to them, our bodies are always with us, making nurturing our soma an easily accessible tool.

Your somatic state tells you a lot about your mind. Paying closer attention to your body can help you learn not only how to better *tend* to your body, but also increase your resilience to burnout. In nurturing your soma, you'll learn ways to practice grounding in your body, connect with spiritual tools such as breath prayer, and much more.

How might tending to your soma invite you to deeper flourishing in your life and relationships?

Engage in Preparation

The P stands for Preparation, which means *make ready before*. It feels a bit uninspired standing alongside the other points of the practice, but preparation is key to being able to wade more deeply into our own flourishing. Preparation is the mental branch of the practice, incorporating emotions but often having an embodied element as well. It draws on setting intentions, practicing mindfulness, and arranging our physical space.

"Prepare" is the word we use in the season of Advent, what we say when we're awaiting the arrival of a child into our lives, and what we draw upon when we're training for a big race. Whether our goal is productivity or rest, we often feel most fulfilled when we take the time to prepare. Like canning food for the long winter ahead, preparation shows tender care and love for our future self.

Focusing on preparation may activate *or* ease your anxiety, so I suggest checking in with yourself about your motivation behind preparing. It is important that preparation doesn't become an idol but a tool that helps you turn your awareness toward the Holy Spirit already at work around you. By spending time preparing, you will be better able to be present in the moment and feel fulfilled in your work and play. A big piece of engaging in preparation is also cultivating compassion, patience, and the skills needed to reset when something doesn't play out according to plan.

What does it look like to prepare your home, your heart, and your life for flourishing?

Make Space for Awe

A is the center point of the SPARK Practice, and it stands for Awe. It's not an accident that awe anchors us, because the practice is grounded around the Holy, or that which is bigger than us. Awe is that sensation we have when we realize we are quite small, and yet are connected into something much bigger. It's the feeling of being a tiny figure standing under the night sky, gazing at the constellations, which precede us by thousands or millions of years. Awe is a positive emotion, and when practiced, it yields even more awe. In other words, awe begets awe.

Through researching awe, psychologist Dacher Keltner and others have found that tapping into awe calms down the nervous system, quiets internal self-criticism, and releases the love hormone oxytocin. Awe makes us want to connect more deeply with our surroundings and communities, while awe's sibling, Wonder, fuels our curiosity. Awe and wonder aren't something you have to go far to find, but they do require you to make space for encountering them. You're especially likely to experience awe and wonder out in creation, when engaging with art or music, or while living out your spirituality.

There are the once-in-a-lifetime Grand Canyon experiences of awe and then the day-to-day moments of witnessing a child interact with an elder or sharing a tender moment with a stranger. Awe has the power to change you for the better, and cultivating awe in connection with the other spokes of the SPARK practice will lead toward flourishing.

How can you orient your life toward more wonder and awe to usher in greater flourishing?

Claim Retreat

R stands for Retreat. Retreat means *to pull back* (v.), or *time set apart* (n.). Retreat incorporates rest and so much more. We must step away to fully engage in the benefit of Retreat. It's necessary for each and every one of us, regardless of our background, and it needn't require a lot of time or money.

Retreat is an ancient practice found across faith backgrounds and cultures. A retreat can take place alone or with a group, in a structured setting or free form, in as little as a minute or longer than a month. In the Christian tradition, we recall Jesus' time spent wandering the wilderness or his retreating to the Garden of Gethsemane to pray. When you embark on retreat, it's often about more than resting, though that is a key component. Retreat is an act of intentional quiet, usually so that you might grow in your self-understanding, relationship with God, or connection with others. Some retreatants go out with a question they're seeking to have answered during this time set apart.

A thirty-second retreat in no less important than a thirty-day retreat. In the Retreat spoke, we will explore the importance of retreat for your wholeheartedness, ways to plan and take time for personal retreat, and how to make retreats more accessible for all.

How can you begin incorporating retreat into all that you do and are, in order that you might make space for flourishing?

Ground Myself in Kinship

K is for Kinship, the ways in which we are inextricably bound to one another and responsible for the flourishing of *all* God's creation. Whether tending to our body (soma), mind (preparation), and spirit (awe), or prioritizing time set apart (retreat), we always return to our interwovenness. Kinship is about not only our connection with others, but also our connection with the earth all around us. It is the daily remembrance that we are not alone, that the way we live our lives impacts one another. It is the acknowledgment that we have been communal creatures from our very beginnings. God did not create us in isolation, but created us in community, along with all of the plants and animals and lands that surround us.

In *Living Resistance*, my friend and author Kaitlin Curtice—member of the Potawatomi Nation—describes kinship as a "string attached to my body, to my heart center, [that] goes directly from my heart to yours, and to every other living creature on this planet, to Mother Earth herself." Kinship is the interconnectedness of all things, as everything we do "travels across that thread" and affects one another. Kinship is a not only a noun, but also a verb: a living, breathing act. We "kin" when we *turn toward* others, when we truly *listen* for what the other needs, and when we *lift up gratitude* for those with whom we share this sacred earth.

Through grounding yourself in kinship, you will learn not only how to grow in your relationships, but to respect the dignity of every living being and remember that you are never alone.

In what ways might you find flourishing by drawing on our interconnectedness?

How to Use This Book

I encourage you to think of this book as not simply an object, but also an experience and a gathering space. When you're here, you're among community. While some might consume it in one sitting, others might sit with it for a season.

You might choose to read this with others or find a partner with whom to wonder aloud. At the close of each chapter, I have included a couple of **reflection questions**. These are for your own self-tending, but I invite you to find a way to share these with others. Something I return to often in this book is that we *must not* go through this life on our own. I encourage you to use these as journal prompts; conversation starters with your therapist, coach, or spiritual director; or a basis for communal sharing with a friend, colleague group, or loved ones.

Reading this may cause you to acknowledge uncomfortable truths. It may take you to places you've tried to avoid. It may turn your life upside down and help you to realize it's time to walk away from something you once loved. So be gentle with yourself and invite others on your journey.

One of my coaching clients refers to her support team as her pit crew: therapist, coach, and spiritual director. This book is intended as a companion, not the sole solution. My hope is that you leave feeling less alone, more refreshed, and better equipped to take on your own flourishing.

Throughout your *From Weary to Wholehearted* journey, you'll notice a soft undercurrent of the liturgical calendar. I draw upon this organic rhythm of the year, but you can read and integrate this resource *in* and *into* any season. We begin with the spiritual themes of justice and anticipation in Advent and move through the long sustaining practices invited by Ordinary Time. My hope is that—while not expressly a homiletic or liturgical resource—this book might also infuse new life into the ministry of weary preachers and leaders.

A Few Terms

It will be unsurprising to most of you that language matters. In fact, researchers have found that using accurate language to talk about what we're experiencing, emotionally and physically, can lead to better self-understanding and reaching out for help when we need it. It also helps us feel less isolated.

I once led a group series on how to move from languishing to flourishing. The best way I knew how to define languishing was to draw on my own experience of a difficult season: "It felt like all of the color saturation had been pulled out of my photos, like I was living as a watercolor version of myself." Deep in languishing, I forgot that there had ever existed a more robust version of me. When I did finally stop to take notice, I remembered a person who laughed easily and danced in the kitchen. And I missed her. I knew that the fullness to which God called me was painted in vibrant colors. But I didn't even know if that was possible again.

Languishing is the feeling of looking through a foggy windshield; it's also categorized by stagnation, lack of focus, and a feeling of disconnectedness. It's that place on the spectrum of mental wellness that is between the valley of depression and the peak of flourishing. Basically, it's a fairly flat plain, and you don't always notice it or have a name for it when you're in it. There's more for you than languishing, dear ones. God envisions singing mountains and clapping rivers (Psalm 98), so certainly God imagines the same for the people who wander this earth. This imagining is a place called flourishing.

In contrast to languishing, **flourishing** is that place where you're thriving in multiple areas of your life. Flourishing is a feeling of accomplishment, flow, and happiness. It's a place where your body, mind, and spirit are aligned, where you can easily be drawn into laughter, song, and dance.

Though languishing often feels like it happens *to* you, flourishing is something you can claim. A lack of flourishing might be caused by overwhelm and burnout. These are used interchangeably, but have distinctions.

Overwhelm occurs when external stressful stimuli are coming in at a faster rate than you can process, leaving you immobilized. Overwhelm can happen in any area of your life.

Burnout refers to overwhelm specifically in the realm of work, however you may define your work. Burnout—coined by Herbert Freudenberger—is a combination of feeling emotionally exhausted, being drained of compassion toward others, and believing that nothing you do makes a difference.

Both overwhelm and burnout require you to pause and to seek support.

I intentionally chose the word **weariness** to encompass a myriad of experiences of stress, overwhelm, burnout, depression, anxiety, and languishing. Weariness is that space you enter when your body and soul feel diminished and in need of rest, but you can't seem to find or claim it.

My invitation to you is wholeheartedness. **Wholeheartedness** is leaning into the belief that you are enough. If you don't think you are worthy of love and belonging, you're not likely to invest the time and energy it takes to live into the fullness of life for which God created you. To be wholehearted is to show up to all your realities: your sorrows and your joys, your brokenness and your healing, your hard seasons and your seasons of thriving. If you are here, I imagine you desire this wholeheartedness.

Since one of my hopes for you is nourishment, consider how and when you engage this book. While writing this gift for you, I intentionally created nourishing space for all of my senses: incense to carry my prayers, tea to warm me through and through, a vinyl record to fill my ears with comfort, cozy blankets to hold me, and a view of the goodness of God's creation outside my windows. Perhaps you want to light a candle or pour a cup of something warm to companion you as you seek your own healing.

Let us begin.

PART
1

Making an Impact

Our shared story begins with a young girl, frightened and alone. Her name is Mary, and the trajectory of her life is about to change forever—and to alter the entire course of history. If you've found your way to this space, you may resonate with Mary. You may feel overwhelmed, uncertain, frightened, or alone. You're in good company, dear ones. Over the course of writing this book, I've had numerous people say, "Oh, please write it quickly! The world so needs this book." I, in turn, had many moments when I felt like Mary must have felt, holding an unimaginably huge responsibility. I wondered if I could possibly do this project the justice it deserved.

In this section, we'll explore what to do when you feel the weight of the world on your shoulders and so often feel immobilized by the task ahead. There is a public-facing nature to our leadership that often feels daunting. And yet, God created us and loved us from the very beginning, in God's very own image. Yes, we are invited to follow Jesus' example of radical love, but first we're invited to follow Mary—bearer of God—and her bravery in the face of uncertainty. We're invited to join Mary in her commitment to cast down the structures that oppress, even when our hands tremble.

1

Waiting on the World to Change

Never forget that justice is what love looks like in public.

—Cornel West

M y neighborhood is filled with artists. It's not uncommon to spot a mural on the side of an abandoned building or to see a tree wearing a knit sweater. A few summers ago, as I walked around the neighborhood, I spotted an art installation along the utility poles. Each post contained a black crocheted heart adorned with flowers and a name in the middle: *Ahmaud. Breonna. George. Trayvon.* All names of Black souls who had been murdered. On the last post was a vintage white doily with red felt lettering. These doilies are a signature of local Philadelphia guerrilla artist Carole Loeffler and usually contain affirmations like *you are loved* or *release fear.* This one said *we are OK,* but instead of a declarative statement, a big red question mark had been added, seemingly as an afterthought: *We are OK?*

What may have started as a word of encouragement transformed into a question most of us have asked ourselves and one another. I see many faith leaders—lay and ordained—struggling to understand our vocational calls in the face of a broken world and a broken institution. I hear people wondering how they might make an impact, whether what they're doing even matters, and how to move past the feeling of helplessness we all experience from time to time (or even daily).

When George Floyd was murdered in early 2020 (as well as Ahmaud Arbery, Breonna Taylor, and countless other Black women and men), I witnessed an increase in leaders questioning their own purpose and impact for good. This was especially true among white leaders, because our Black, Indigenous, and People of Color (BIPOC) siblings were by and large unsurprised by the violence against Black and Brown bodies, and mistrustful of the long-lasting impact of a social uprising or revolution. Many white leaders—including myself—found themselves wondering what kind of influence they had, how to use their power and privilege to help bring about God's Reign of Peace, and—if leading a congregation—how their people might join in or push back. Simultaneously, many BIPOC leaders described being exhausted by continually having to carry the load, while also being triggered anew by racial injustice.

As you watch the world fall apart and come back together, again and again, through oppression, hate, war, and poverty, you might find yourself wondering how to mend your own broken heart and how to make sense of it for those whom you lead. You may feel the need to respond immediately to every single crisis, or you may feel guilty when you don't. Faith leaders receive mixed messages, some saying, "if you don't preach on this current issue, you are not worthy to call yourself a leader," and others pleading, "can't we just stick to the Bible?" It can all feel overwhelming.

Even if you choose to opt out of the twenty-four-hour news cycle and decline the responsibility of carrying the woes of the world, you can't fully escape the brokenness in the Church as an institution. While the Church is a place that is intended to model the gospel of good news to the oppressed, it often instead perpetuates hate, discrimination, and abuse. Many faith leaders have witnessed, or have first-hand experience of, the toxicity of the institution, for which there often seems to be little to no recourse.

When I began writing this book, I asked sibling clergy about their biggest source of weariness and burnout. With-out contest, the answers were systemic—particularly, wide-spread sexism and misogyny ("the patriarchy"), racism, and heterosexism. Those leaders who are not white, cis-gendered men generally report having a harder time in ministry, from additional barriers in the ordination process to difficulty finding positions with adequate pay—and, going beyond, to how they're treated by colleagues, supervisors, and congre-gants. Whether you have experienced this kind of imped-iment to your flourishing, you are aware that the Church tenets and scripture have been used to justify everything from slavery to conversion (anti-gay) therapy. At the hand of the Church, partners experiencing domestic violence have been encouraged to stay in their relationships. Under the watch of the Church, children who should have been learn-ing about God's love have suffered abuse. In the name of the Church, families have been supported in disowning their LGBTQ+ children.

We cannot unsee all of that. Not to put too fine a point on it, but a Body that has caused hurt in the past has a dif-ficult time reclaiming its identity as a place for healing. We cannot simply wait for the world to change on its own. This responsibility often falls on church leaders. And yet, it can be difficult to change a world that is actively causing you harm. You must also care for your own selves and seek your own healing first.

We are okay? Dear ones, we are not. We are weary, and we don't often know where to turn with that weariness.

Over the past several years of offering ministry coaching and spiritual companioning, I've noticed a trend. My practice grows in seasons of societal turmoil: global pandemic, war, racial reckoning. It is in those moments when people most question their purpose, feel lost, or wonder if they're capable of influencing change for good. Even if someone was content not to disrupt the status quo before, they no longer feel like they can stand idly by. As people of faith bear witness to protests and rebellions, many feel a spark ignite in themselves. Perhaps it's a spark of righteous anger, a spark of discomfort, or the teeniest, tiniest flame that they don't know how to tend to, but which tells them that they need to do something different.

Regardless of the source of oppression, some peacemakers—a term used by Black pastor and author Osheta Moore to invite white Christians into the work of anti-racism—say the messages they hear are confusing:

Sit down and listen.
Stand up and speak.

When we experience conflicting messages—internally or externally—we tend to stand motionless. Instead of working toward change, we remain immobilized. Whether you're just beginning the work of dismantling oppression and addressing abusive structures of power, or whether you have been engaging in this work for years, it's important to educate yourself, confess our societal and your individual wrongdoing, and walk alongside our siblings whose lives are at stake. You may be worried about saying the wrong thing or not saying enough. But the voices of our neighbors, colleagues, and friends cry out for us to show up and to stop perpetuating violence toward them.

We must speak up even if we mess up and get called out for it. We're not going to get it right every time, but we must start somewhere; each miss is a chance to learn, receive grace, and try again.

If you find yourself in need of an anchor, there is goodness ahead. In chapter 2, we'll acknowledge and embrace the complexities of life and emotion, and in chapter 3, we'll claim our part in casting down the mighty.

Reflection Questions

In what ways have you felt overwhelmed by the brokenness in the world and the institution of the Church? How has this impacted your understanding of your vocation?

How do you navigate the tension between the urge to respond to every crisis and the feeling of guilt when not responding? What practices or boundaries have you put in place to care for your own well-being while still engaging with the issues of the world?

Discuss a moment when you felt called to "sit down and listen" versus a moment you felt urged to "stand up and speak." What discernment did you use to decide, and how did it align with your values and the needs of those you serve?

2

A Place for Despair

For everything there is a season and a time for every matter
under heaven:
a time to be born and a time to die;
a time to plant and a time to pluck up what is planted;
a time to kill and a time to heal;
a time to break down and a time to build up;
a time to weep and a time to laugh;
a time to mourn and a time to dance;
a time to throw away stones and a time to gather
stones together;
a time to embrace and a time to refrain from embracing;
a time to seek and a time to lose;
a time to keep and a time to throw away;
a time to tear and a time to sew;
a time to keep silent and a time to speak;
a time to love and a time to hate;
a time for war and a time for peace.

—Ecclesiastes 3:1–8

t's okay to not be okay.
I have a scar that resides between my eyebrows, just
above the bridge of my nose. A few years ago, a photographer friend asked about it. The story itself isn't too
exciting—I fell forehead-first into the corner of a coffee

table when I was a toddler—but her question brought up another memory for me.

When I had senior portraits taken in high school, my photographer offered to edit out my scar. I couldn't understand what he meant. I'd had that same scar almost my entire life. To edit it out would be to pretend I was someone I wasn't.

We do that a lot, though. We gloss over the hard stuff in favor of what we perceive to be good. But who exactly gets to determine what is good?

The Church and society both emphasize light, hope, peace, and joy. But what happens when the people around you simply can't access those states? What happens when it's you who can't arrive at light, hope, peace, and joy?

During a clergy quiet day, I introduced the idea of a shadow to the brightness of each Advent candle. Over the course of Advent, we light four candles in anticipation of Christ's coming. We often refer to these candles as Hope, Peace, Joy (*Gaudete!*), and Love. Perhaps we strive to live into those things here and now, but I believe we also light them as symbols of a world we imagine to be possible when Jesus comes back to earth—a world where hope, peace, joy, and love will reign. Until then, as I go through the succession of lighting those candles each year, I understand how important it is to not only uplift these positive emotions, but to integrate what we might think of as the shadow of each of these candles: despair, chaos, lament, and heartache.

As leaders, you may feel the need to exude a hopey-changey attitude in all that you do, but our reality is much less straightforward. The concepts of hope, peace, joy, and love contain a deeper complexity which, when honored, contributes to the wholeness of each. They exist in relationship with despair, chaos, lament, and heartache. We need to be able to acknowledge this reality for our own weary selves, and others need us to model it boldly. In the shadows, there's plenty of perspective, growth, and even beauty to be found. By focusing on the fullness held within each candle, people have permission to embrace the whole spectrum of their feelings, freedom to not ignore their emotions or place them in a box.

Years ago, I developed a *"Finding Nemo* Theory of Hard Things."* In the Pixar animated film, a clown fish named Marlin swims the ocean looking for his lost son Nemo. While out there, he befriends a forgetful fish named Dory. As Marlin and Dory are approaching a rather treacherous area, Dory gets advice from local fish to swim *through* the trench, not over it. Her memory predictably fails her as they arrive at the trench, but nevertheless, she tries to warn Marlin to swim through the trench. Marlin dismisses her, saying "It's got death written all over it," and they try skirting the danger by swimming over the trench.

Unsurprisingly, in their efforts to avoid the scary thing, they end up in a patch of jellyfish and get seriously injured. I have learned to take Dory's intuition to heart when I'm encountering grief or something difficult: "I think we should swim through it, not over it." When we try to bypass the hard stuff of life, it never seems to work. We either get hurt in the process of avoidance, or we find that—in the end— we must go through the hard thing anyway.

Let's look at what we might find in each of the companion candles for Advent.

Hope and Despair

We have hope *because* of the times we've survived, because of the times when we longed for a light at the end of the tunnel and it finally arrived. Hope is born of struggle. It's born from the times we've persisted. Surely, there are plenty of times when our hopes are dashed, and those can make us wary of daring to hope again. And yet, we are creatures oriented toward hope.

On the other side of hope is *hopelessness* or *despair*. Our hopelessness tends to be focused on the present state of things. Despair, on the other hand, encompasses how we feel about our future as well. Theologian Rob Bell says that despair is the "belief that tomorrow will be just like today." It can make us feel like we're in a never-ending loop, like we're stuck.

I've watched many people reside in the shadow of hope: wondering if a pregnancy will remain viable after numerous losses, or whether an old conflict with a coworker will find a new way to crop up. They've often said to me that they're too afraid to hope, that they've experienced too much loss to believe that it won't happen again. Even when we can't hold hope, we can ask others to hold hope alongside us.

Peace and Chaos

A complete view of the concept of peace contains both communal and individual elements. We begin by focusing on the peace that resides within us, what we might call a sense of grounding or calm. While it's tempting to want to walk through the world in a constant state of zen, it is neither possible nor helpful to do so. In *Leadership and the New Science*, Margaret Wheatley argues that chaos is a prerequisite to transformation. Chaos is natural and rather impossible to avoid. When we're in states of chaos, it helps our brain adapt and it even strengthens our heart. Persevering through chaos is generative.

Chaos requires that we think outside of the box, that we get creative. Without the presence of chaos, we continue to do things the way they've always been done, which certainly doesn't help bring about necessary change.

Chaos can disrupt our lives. But that disruption can lead to a new and deeper peace. A living room dance party with my beloveds is anything but peaceful. There's typically music blaring and lots of movement, and our pups often add their voices to the cacophony. Some days, I want to cover my ears and hide in a corner. But on others, I realize this is truly the Holy Spirit at work in my home and my heart, opening me up to deeper joy and fulfillment. Chaos can be both beautiful and transformative.

Joy and Lament

Joy may be lovely, but it can also be toxic. One of the many things I love about the church seasons in my tradition are that some are set aside for quieter contemplation, and some are set aside for unbridled jubilation.

One way I've seen the church world embrace the complexities of the Advent season is by hosting a Blue Christmas service. A Blue Christmas service is open to anyone, but is especially targeted toward those who have experienced loss and are having a hard time finding the "Christmas spirit." It's a powerful experience to sit in a sacred space and have permission to grieve, or to know that anger is welcome.

The shadow of joy—lament—comes from a place of anguish, sadness, or grief. While each of these emotions is different, they can pave the way for a need of lamentation. Lamentation is the way we externally express those deep feelings and has precedent in Hebrew scripture, particularly in the Book of Lamentations and in many of the psalms.

The experience of anguish invites us to connect with one another, whether we share the same source of anguish or draw upon our own times of profound sadness.

Love and Heartache

As a parent, I hate watching one of my children have their heart broken or their hopes dashed. I want to cover them in bubble wrap and protect their hearts, but my role isn't to protect them from the hard parts of life. It's to show up alongside them when they find themselves in those hard parts. It is through experiencing heartache that we treasure love more deeply.

Love is a great act of vulnerability. The only way to truly avoid heartbreak is to avoid sharing our heart with another. It's quite courageous to risk love.

By allowing ourselves to love and allowing ourselves to embrace heartache when it comes our way, we honor the fullness of our humanity.

So, how do we integrate these shadows into our spirituality and leadership? First, we must believe that the entirety of human experience is valuable. We must believe that God chose to dwell among us not simply to experience pleasure and joy, but also pain and hurt. And we must let go of the illusion that to lead well is to constantly be in a positive mental and spiritual space.

I'm the person who pulls over on the side of the road at a moment's notice to photograph fall leaves. I can't help it; their radiance makes my heart leap in awe of God's creation, and I want some lasting evidence of their fleeting existence. What I hear again and again during autumn is that there's beauty in letting go. Perhaps, for you, letting go looks like breathtaking transformation followed by a time to rest and regrow. Perhaps it's a little bit messier. But what would it look like to let go of some of the ways of being and leading that aren't serving you and instead embrace a more holistic self?

I once had the immense honor of joining Thistle Farms in Nashville for their weekly meditation circle. This organization has walked alongside countless women as they've left behind lives of addiction and embarked on a journey to recover from sex trafficking. As I listened to stories from graduates of the program, tears sprang from my eyes. These women leaned into their "not okay." When they took the step to join Thistle Farms, they acknowledged that they wanted to stop hurting, make different choices, and that they needed help. In this circle, it was okay to not be okay. Over time, through their own bravery, the support of one another, and the strength of God, they found healing.

It's okay to not be okay, dear ones. Your hurts are real, even if they're old wounds. Your emotions are normal, even if they're inconvenient. You don't have to grip so tightly.

Reflection Questions

In moments when you feel disconnected from hope, peace, joy, and love, how do you honor feelings of despair, chaos, lament, and heartache in your personal life and ministry?

Reflect on a time when embracing the "shadow" of a positive emotion (like hope or joy) provided you with greater understanding or growth. How did this experience influence your approach to leadership and pastoral care?

3

Rise Up

Arise, shine, for your light has come, and the glory of the Lord has risen upon you.

—*Isaiah 60:1*

I n my first year of college, I was reading through the student newspaper when something caught my eye: an ad promising lucrative returns for stuffing envelopes. I fantasized about how many envelopes I could stuff while watching TV, recalling many afternoons spent helping my church administrator mom with collating, folding, and mailing newsletters. I was so hooked by the idea of making fast cash that I overlooked the fact that there would most certainly be a catch. What was billed as envelope stuffing was actually a pyramid scheme wherein I would pay a small initial fee and then recruit family and friends to take advantage of the same opportunity. Things don't usually just *happen* without personal investment or cost.

There is an often-toxic movement referred to as *manifestation—if we think positive thoughts, positive things will happen.* Manifestation is a commonly used word in the world of spiritual wellness. It goes like this: What can we manifest if we but speak the words into the universe or wish it deeply enough? Manifesting something is simply thinking or speaking a desire and having it come true, like "I want to be in a serious relationship by this time next year" or "I intend to make that cute little beach bungalow my own, even though it's not for sale." We hear about the desires that come to bear fruit, but not so much about the ones that fall short.

It's an enticing prospect, but much like the ad I read in my college paper, manifestation has a catch. Speaking our dreams into the world is always a beautiful thing, but when they don't come to life, some of us may wonder if we prayed hard enough, if we weren't deserving enough, or if we did something wrong. Manifestation often overlooks privilege— the advantage people in positions of power (i.e., men, white folks, cisgendered individuals) often have assigned to them without even having to work for it. To speak a desire out loud and have it become a reality is a lot easier when we have money, professional networks, influence, and power. Since manifestation and privilege often go hand in hand, to name one without the other is problematic at best and, frankly, quite dangerous at its worst.

While manifestation has its problems, it can also be destructive to keep your dreams small and your beliefs to yourself. We are called into a wholeness of life, which means honoring our dreams and working to create a world where the dreams of *all* God's children are realized. We can approach life with the full understanding of what our particular experience brings to bear, acknowledging that there are things in this world beyond our control, *while also making* a conscious decision to rise. In the midst of the despair and chaos of this world, we are called to rise. We are called to name aloud the brokenness we experience and witness, while breaking down the structures that oppress others at the same time.

As leaders, we have both a charge and a privilege. In our settings—churches, hospitals, schools, and more—people look to us to guide them through times of despair. Some of them want us to make sense of it all, which is never an easy task.

Systemic issues of heterosexism, racism, misogyny, classism, and ableism are pressing in hard around us and our ministries. Let's return for a moment to that young woman who belonged to the working class of centuries past: Mary, mother of God. Though she was seen as powerless by many, Mary had autonomy over her situation. She decided to stand tall and speak her heart. In the Magnificat, Mary proclaims, "[The Lord] has brought down the powerful from their thrones and lifted up the lowly; he has filled the hungry with good things and sent the rich away empty."

Part of taking care of ourselves is paving the way for justice for all people. Let's show up and be bold like Mary. Let's help make a dent in the oppressive structures for our own sake and for the sake of all of God's beloveds.

Who am I to speak up? Who am I to make a difference? You are exactly the one, because you're the trusted leader, the trusted partner, the trusted friend, and people often first encounter God's message of radical love through an individual whom they trust. You have innumerable gifts, and your voice is valuable and needed.

Part of being wholehearted is to show up with our whole entire being, for ourselves, for our neighbors and strangers, and for God. In sociologist Brené Brown's research on people who show up bravely and vulnerably to their lives, she sought a label to categorize these individuals. While she was in church praying the confession—"we have not loved you with our whole heart"—she realized that *wholehearted* was the perfect categorization. Through this prayer of whole-hearted confession, we acknowledge our communal sins—those things done and left undone—before God.

I invite you to look at this prayer more closely and reflect on what it might mean to be wholehearted:

We have not loved you with our whole heart
We have not loved our neighbors as ourselves
We are truly sorry and we humbly repent

We have not loved you with our whole heart. To be whole-hearted means not watching out only for ourselves and our own best interests, but weeping with Rachel for her dead children in Ramah, overturning the tables of injustice, and standing alongside the widow and orphan, outcast and stranger.

We have not loved our neighbors as ourselves. To be whole-hearted means when one of us is broken, none of us is whole. We are broken, dear ones. Actions borne out of the sins of privilege and hate literally kill our siblings and our children. When we don't understand or acknowledge the ways we each have implicit advantages over one another, we can't work to equalize the imbalance.

We are truly sorry and we humbly repent. To be whole-hearted means to name the ways we've hurt one another or remained complicit. To repent is to turn. We are charged with turning our attention to God's children—whose world is on fire—and declaring with our words and actions that they matter.

God has created each and every one of us in God's own image. Let us love God with our whole heart by bravely and boldly allowing that principle to guide our lives. We can wait—in hope—for the world to change, but we are empowered and strengthened to follow in the example of

Mary, casting down the mighty and filling the hungry with good things.

Reflection Questions

In the context of systemic issues like racism, sexism, and classism, how do you balance the call to "arise and shine" with the need for self-care and personal restoration?

Reflect on the last time you truly felt wholehearted in your ministry. What does it mean for you to "love with your whole heart," and how can you cultivate this in your day-to-day life?

Part 1
SPARK Practice

See pp. xvii–xxiii for an introduction to the SPARK Practice.

nurture my **S**oma
engage in **P**reparation
make space for **A**we
claim **R**etreat
ground myself in **K**inship

Soma: Know Your Physiology

During a training on shame resilience, I was led in an exercise where the group portrayed the physiology of shame by marking up a gingerbread figure on easel paper. One by one, we added onto the figure the places we personally experience shame. By the time everyone pinpointed their shame, the paper gingerbread person was covered in marker and looking rather anguished. Their throat was closed off, their armpits tingly, their ears radiating heat, their heart pumping, their legs shaking, their stomach turning. Your body can tell you a great deal about your emotions.

Scan your body. Perhaps the simplest way to start taking note of what your soma might be telling you is to do a body scan meditation. Get as quiet as possible, deepen your breath, and—starting at the top of your head—slowly and intentionally check in with each part of your body.

Where am I holding tension? Where am I at ease? You might lower your shoulders or unclench your jaw as you move down and discover areas where you're housing your stress.

Get to know your physiological signs. For me, I know I'm in a state of shame (as opposed to anger or grief) when I lower my head, avoid eye contact, and sometimes even want to retreat and pull the literal covers over my head. Learning the somatic indicators of your emotions can help you identify them more quickly and respond to them more compassionately.

Preparation: Intention

Several years ago, I realized that many of our Jewish siblings don't simply stop everything and take a day of Sabbath rest on Saturdays, but rather engage in the intentional work of preparation throughout the week. In order to not cook on the Sabbath, they prepare meals ahead of time. In order to not drive, they run their errands during the week. In order to not use electricity, they pre-program the lights. All of the ways in which they are able to rest rely upon them symbolically setting the table in advance. Preparation may not feel like the most compelling spoke of this practice, but it is key to cultivating presence, mindfulness, and true rest. Whether you're getting ready for your sabbath day, a vacation, or a retreat, how do you build in intentional time for preparation?

Awe: Morning Light

There's a lot I don't know right now. But here's what I do know: Every morning, the sun comes up over the horizon.

The light shines forth once more. Night does not last forever. It never has. It never will. Every morning, I marvel at the thing my partner and I call "hopeful morning light." Winter or summer, come rain or shine, every single morning the sun rises again. No matter what the preceding day held, there's a chance to begin again.

A few years ago, I picked up a coffee table book at the cabin I rented for my solo retreat. It talked about three practices for each day, revolving around the light of the sun: a morning practice of standing in the first light for at least one minute, a midday practice of soaking up the sun for at least thirty minutes (perhaps an outdoor lunch or a walk), and a day-ending practice of letting sunset be the last significant light of the day and relying on lamp and candlelight in the evening to wind down toward sleep. I don't always incorporate all of these practices into my day, but the one that remains most helpful is immersing myself in the hopeful morning light. Here's what it looks like: As early in the day as possible, go out into the morning light, orient yourself toward the sun, and breathe in the air. You can connect this to a gratitude practice as well, giving thanks for a fresh new day and all it will bring.

Retreat: Pausing

At my ordination, my bishop asked me, "My sister, do you believe that you are truly called by God and God's Church to this priesthood?" And I answered, "I believe I am so called." Every day, I strive to uphold those promises and the many others I made that day. I try to set aside time to study scripture and to focus on prayer. But the reality is, those things don't always happen. If we aren't paying close attention, the stuff of life gets in the way of following our purpose and tending to our souls.

Some people I know have retreats scheduled quarterly, while others have never been on a retreat at all. I wonder if you've taken a pause? There's something unkind—I think it's fear—that tells us now is the time to keep pushing onward, that now is *not* the time for rest. When you hear that message, it's precisely the time to pause, to be reminded of your belovedness, and to gather what you need before continuing the journey.

Take a few moments to identify the last time you took a retreat. Whether it's retreating to the sanctuary you build in your mind or packing up and getting out of town, what do you need to be able to take a pause?

Kinship: Belonging(s)

One of my favorite writing spots is on our sunporch. It's a space my partner and I built with our own hands, and it houses our vinyl collection, so it is the incarnation of creativity. It also looks out to our yard and neighboring trees, and when the doors and windows are open, the space fills with sounds of birdsong and chirping insects. Each piece of furniture has been carefully chosen, including the vintage, hope-symbolizing hanging egg chair that I bought before we ever even built the frame for the room. But under my feet sits perhaps the most significant item: a simple wooden footstool with a hand-stitched leather cushion. I claimed it from my mom's house as she was downsizing, thinking of it as classy and utilitarian. It was only as I was putting it in my space that I learned it had belonged to my great-grandmother. To have my feet supported by this heirloom made me feel deeply connected to and uplifted by my namesake.

Look around your space at your belongings and name the things which connect you to others. Perhaps it's the maker of the object, the one who gave it to you, or the one to whom it once belonged. We are connected, one to another.

A Prayer
for Rising

O Bearer of Despair and Hope,
be present with us in our breadth and depth
of human experience.
Help us cast down the mighty,
even when the mighty is us.
May we not wait
but bring about change
in our weary and broken world,
today and each new day.
For ourselves,
for our siblings,
for those souls with whom our paths will never cross.
In tenderness and strength we pray,
Amen.

2

Feeling Seen and Finding Belonging

We are weary, dear ones. Our work as faith leaders can leave us feeling isolated and misunderstood. Many of us got into this work because we love the gospel, love the liturgy, love encountering the Holy in community. Even so, being in ministry often means we're cultivating that experience for others and leaving little time and space to encounter it ourselves.

Every year since I've been in ministry, people ask me what my plans are for Christmas or Easter. I have to restrain myself from gesturing broadly and saying, "I make this whole thing happen." It is one of the greatest honors of my life to invite people into the sacred experiences of incarnation and resurrection, but I am keenly aware that those in the pews and those serving around the altar have different experiences of the Church. One is not good or better, but many clergy I work with describe answering the call to ministry precisely because of their encounters with the Holy in a communal faith setting, only to lose the experience of those encounters within the context of their vocations.

We pour immense energy into creating a space of belonging for others, yet may not feel that belonging ourselves.

Medical professionals who provide healing still need healing themselves. Mental health professionals need their own care provider to maintain their own well-being. And ministry professionals who create space where others know love in the context of community? They too need to know and feel love in community.

In this section, we'll dive into the isolation of leading a spiritual community or providing care for others while not always having that community or care for ourselves. Within the context of incarnation, we'll explore what it means to be made *imago dei* (in God's own image), the ways in which we are already enough, and how the practices of empathy and self-compassion can help us feel more understood and less isolated.

CHAPTER

4

In the Beginning

Then God said, "Let us make humankind in our image, according to our likeness."

—*Genesis 1:26*

The light shines in the darkness, and the darkness did not overtake it.

—*John 1:5*

asy like Sunday morning? Whoever said this is clearly *not* parish clergy, let alone a clergy parent. Here's a glimpse into what my Sunday mornings looked like as a parish priest when my children were young: getting both kids up and dressed in their Sunday *better*— no Sunday best in our household. If it was clean-ish, it was acceptable. We were lucky to get out of the house on time, and breakfast was leftover pancakes from home, warmed up in the church kitchen. One Sunday, I recall getting more comments on my nail polish than my sermon, and my then-five-year-old made pencil drawings on the pew while I was up front celebrating the Eucharist. I wouldn't exactly describe Sunday morning as *easy*.

I wouldn't describe anything about the vocation of a ministry professional as easy. As faith leaders, our jobs *and* our personal lives often feel like they're on public display.

We wear many hats, fill many roles, and have many expectations placed upon us. Whether we're working multiple jobs, parenting, caring for elders, or more, our attention is split between numerous things on any given day. Each vocation seems to demand our full attention. Partners, children, pets, friends, congregants . . . when we're with them, they want all of us, not a piece of our whole self. So, no, nothing about this is easy.

And yet, I can't say I went into any of this looking for easy. Fulfilling? Yes. Transformative? Definitely. My vocations as a mama and a priest certainly aren't a walk in the park. Sometimes I fall short of expectations (usually self-imposed), sometimes there's weeping and gnashing of teeth (usually my own), and sometimes it feels like thankless work. All of that is true. But what if we aren't called into easy? What if we're called into real?

When you are living out that thing into which the Holy invites you, it's going to challenge you. You're going to show up with your whole self, your whole imperfect self. You might struggle to make it all the way up the challenging hill and instead want to sit down right there with your arms crossed, refusing to take one more step.

There are some truths I invite you to live into in those moments. They don't make the hard stuff go away, but they certainly make it feel less lonely. The first truth is that God shaped you from the very beginning. During the days following Christmas, one of my favorite things to do is to come downstairs when the sun is still sleeping and turn on nothing but the soft light of the tree. It's in these intimate and peaceful moments that I can reflect on being created from beautiful, glorious darkness. I can recall that I'm a small part of something so much bigger. I can be assured that God abides in me and nothing I do or don't do changes that. Honestly, it takes some of the pressure off needing to show up perfectly in my vocations.

The second truth is that you are made *imago dei*—in God's very own image. Are there hundreds of thousands of self-help books out there intended to make you a better pastor, parent, partner, or global citizen? Absolutely. Do you need any of those books in order to be claimed as God's own for ever and ever? No. That fact is woven into the very fabric of your being. You may not always feel like you belong. Perhaps you feel the tension between your many vocations and the way they sometimes seem to be at odds with one another. You might feel assured in your call to lead but still want spaces where you can simply dwell. The multiple hats you wear, the many jobs you hold, the numerous directions in which you feel pulled, are all iterations of the Divine.

The third truth—so deeply related to the first two—is that you are enough. There will be plenty of moments when you don't feel understood or respected, by folks within your ministry setting and also your friends and family. You will inevitably try to carry far too many plates and will drop a few. You will likely step on toes and have your toes stepped on. Even and especially then, you are still worthy of love and belonging. There is a deep correlation between ministry leaders and childhood trauma—many go into this vocation to help bring healing to others and to heal the wounds of their past. Some days, the voices of not-enoughness may be impossibly loud. You may feel like you need to prove yourself or make people like you again and again and again. You don't. In those seasons, I invite you to rest in your enoughness.

Our vocation is at turns heart-rending and beautiful. Perhaps you're struggling in this season or perhaps you're thriving. I see you showing up and living into your vocation(s). I see you striving to be your best and to show up authentically. It certainly is not easy. There are the moments when we persevere anyway. Those are often the moments when light breaks in through the cracks, and when transformation can happen.

Those Sunday mornings when my tossed-into-the-car children sat alone in the pews while I tried my best to concentrate on the liturgy up front? God was praised by toddlers in the congregation who loudly proclaimed the Lord's Prayer. The Holy Spirit showed up as I served the bread and wine to the broken-hearted and to the joyous. Jesus was present as I spent coffee hour discussing how to solve the US border crisis over lemonade and cookies.

We are all susceptible to coming down with a case of *the Shoulds*. The Shoulds happen when you're filled with self-blame and comparison, and you find yourself reviewing all the things you *should* have done differently or better. *I should have responded more firmly, I should have completed that task sooner, I should have* . . . This type of review is different from self-reflection, which can lead to positive change; the Shoulds just keep us frozen in place. The Shoulds are related to that nagging inner voice that tells you that you aren't doing enough, producing enough, earning enough, being enough. I teach on comparison and preach on grace, but—alas!—even I am not immune to the Shoulds.

Throughout my ministry, I've regularly come down with a case of the Shoulds. My symptoms usually include shame and negative self-talk. I find myself stealing glances at others and wondering why I'm not handling the stress of the season as well, or parenting as calmly, or working as efficiently as others seem to be. The Shoulds come on quickly and can be hard to shake. But the cure for the Shoulds is the Ams. I mean this in three ways: First, instead of focusing on what you should have done, focus on what you *are* doing and accomplishing. Second, practice some truth-telling: I am strong, I am loving, I am thoughtful, I am a beloved child of God. Finally, remember that you don't have to do it all, because there's the great I AM (God, through Jesus): I am the bread of life, the light of the world, the true vine.

What would happen if you were to shift the Shoulds into the Ams? You can do this by speaking or seeking affirmation of yourself, by connecting to God in nature, by tapping into your creativity, or by taking yourself less seriously. If it's unfamiliar or your practice is rusty, try this: I am good, I am enough, I am worthy of love and belonging.

Reflection Questions

Reflect on the moments when your vocational responsibilities feel overwhelming and public. How do you navigate the expectations placed upon you, and what practices help you to remain grounded in your identity as God's beloved?

Recall a moment when you experienced the Holy Spirit working through the imperfections of life, such as a chaotic Sunday or an unexpected interruption. How did this moment reveal the presence of God in your midst?

CHAPTER

5

Indwelling of Love

"Look, the virgin shall become pregnant and give birth to
a son, and they shall name him Emmanuel," which means,
"God is with us."

—*Matthew 1:23*

I pray that, according to the riches of his glory, he may grant
that you may be strengthened in your inner being with
power through his Spirit and that Christ may dwell in your
hearts through faith, as you are being rooted and grounded
in love. I pray that you may have the power to comprehend,
with all the saints, what is the breadth and length and
height and depth and to know the love of Christ that sur-
passes knowledge, so that you may be filled with all the fullness of God.

—*Ephesians 3:16–19*

I first met **Tina at a retreat** I led on Lake Tahoe. Despite
her many decades of life, Tina hadn't ever truly heard the
message that she is beloved and that she is enough. Even
when our group of supportive women said this to Tina, she
met us with an incredulous look. Tina has a laugh that peals
through a room, and her voice gets really soft when tears
spring to her eyes. She is also deathly afraid of water. But
over the course of our retreat weekend, something happened.

Tina began to believe that she was indeed made in God's image. Maybe not fully, but something shifted in Tina. Her excitement burst forth, and her confidence emerged. She said, "I think I want to try kayaking."

Two incredible things happened here. First, Tina claimed her enoughness. She decided she was tired of always opting out and instead wanted to opt in. She wanted to look her fears in the face and say, "Nope, not today." Every negative message that she had absorbed since childhood, and then carried inside into adulthood, loosened its grip ever so slightly. Instead of living into a narrative of limitation—one where Tina recalled all the ways she falls short or misses out—she showed herself deep love and compassion.

The second incredible thing to happen was this: Another participant piped up and said to Tina, "I'll go with you." That person *also* put on a life jacket and climbed into the boat. This is the best image I can conjure up for empathy. Empathy—to feel *with*—is different from sympathy—to feel *for*. Sympathy would have been standing on the shoreline watching Tina bob away. Empathy is climbing in the boat. It's the only way to truly see from another's perspective.

Thousands of years ago, God climbed into the boat. God chose to come down to earth to dwell as a human, not cheering us on from the shoreline, but abiding in and among us. Incarnation is the greatest act of empathy I can imagine. The incarnation of Love—God coming to this earth in the form of a human—is something that never ceases to amaze me. The idea that God wanted to know us better, to understand us more deeply, to experience the depth and breadth of human emotion firsthand, is so incredibly compelling to me.

I recently read that, upon birth, animals immediately do what's needed for survival: A baby giraffe takes their first steps, which is necessary to avoid becoming prey. Upon being born, a human cries. I imagine Jesus did as well, despite the claim to the contrary in "Silent Night." Human babies cry because what's needed for our survival is support from others. When Jesus was born into this world, God took on the greatest form of vulnerability and embodied dependence. God also took on laughter that knocks us out of our chair and sorrow that brings us to our knees. God became Emmanuel—*God with us*—so that God might know the deep range of human emotion.

Empathy and self-compassion are two of the ways we can most clearly mirror and experience God's love through Jesus. Empathy is related to compassion and is the act of understanding another's emotions and trying to take their perspective. While we might never experience the same things as another person, we can all connect through shared emotions. I've never lost a sibling, but I have lost a parent, so I can connect with the experience of grief after the death of a loved one. A couple of important components to practicing empathy are perspective-taking—putting yourself in someone else's shoes and imagining what they might need—and mindfulness—the idea of sitting with an emotion, even if it's negative, without feeling that you need to move toward fixing it.

Empathy and self-compassion are two sides of the same coin; the difference lies in whether the experience of *feeling with* is directed internally or externally. While I could offer a lengthy introduction to the concept of self-compassion, I've found that one sobering question can identify self-compassion: Have I been speaking to myself as I would speak to a loved one?

When I ask this question, people tend to get really quiet. I watch as they swallow hard. Then, they usually glance down and utter a soft "no." The truth is that it's rough out there in the world. Our days are long and our struggles are plentiful. I believe that we would all deeply benefit from a long nap and a big hug. But we also need to practice self-compassion. Only you can show yourself self-compassion, and self-compassion has the power not only to give you strength in the present but also to heal your past wounds.

Empathy is sitting with others when things are hard. Self-compassion is sitting with yourself when things are hard. To practice these is to honor the Incarnation and to make sure we all feel seen and heard.

I once led a weekend intensive on living wholeheartedly, introducing our time with a quote from Brené Brown that explained wholeheartedness in part as believing that we are worthy of love and belonging:

> Wholehearted living is about engaging with our lives from a place of worthiness. It means cultivating the courage, compassion and connection to wake up in the morning and think, "No matter what gets done and how much is left undone, I am enough." It's going to bed at night thinking, "Yes, I am imperfect and vulnerable and sometimes afraid, but that doesn't change the truth that I am also brave and worthy of love and belonging."

During our three days, I led brave men and women through trust and vulnerability, empathy and self-compassion, shame, resilience, and more. As our time together came to a close, I asked what practices the participants wanted to take home with them. There were many rich and inspiring answers, and then one participant vulnerably and honestly admitted she didn't imagine she'd put any of this into practice at home. I said, "Remember on the first night when we talked about believing you are worthy of love and belonging? I wonder if you're there yet." She said she wasn't. With great empathy, I said I could imagine it would be difficult to bring home practices to work on when you don't yet believe the basic building blocks of love and belonging. Without that foundation, we're unlikely to invest in ourselves.

As you dive deeper into your journey of nourishment and flourishing, I invite you to rest in the truths that God has come to this earth so that God might know you more fully, and that you are already enough.

There will always be times in our vocations when we question ourselves or speak to ourselves unkindly. We must ground ourselves in self-compassion and surround ourselves with others who will show us empathy. You are already enough, and God is already dwelling in you.

Reflection Questions

How do you practice empathy in your ministry and personal life? Can you share a moment when you chose to "climb into the boat" with someone rather than standing on the shoreline? Who has done that for you?

Reflect on a time when you, like Tina, chose to face a fear or challenge by deciding to "opt in" rather than "opt out." What shifted within you when you made that choice?

Part 2
SPARK Practice

nurture my **S**oma
engage in **P**reparation
make space for **A**we
claim **R**etreat
ground myself in **K**inship

Soma: Movement

In my thirties, recently divorced and committed to figuring out my identity, I wanted to find ways to nurture myself and step outside of my comfort zone. One of the things I did was to take a hip-hop dance class. Am I coordinated? No. Do I look ridiculous trying to learn new moves and string them together? Probably. Was it fun? *Yes.* Movement is about so much more than burning calories. The number one stress buster is physical activity. Movement has been shown to have physical and mental benefits, and I know many—including myself—who use some form of movement as a spiritual practice as well. Movement doesn't have to look like what your neighbor is doing for weight loss, and it certainly doesn't need to break the bank or any records.

Try something new or something you enjoy. Movement need not feel like punishment! Meet up with a friend for a stroll, join a group class, or dance your heart out to your favorite playlist. Anything that causes you to breathe deeply again will do.

Preparation: Truth-Telling

One day as I was getting ready for a big meeting, I felt a wave of anxiety come over me. I didn't know how the meeting would go, and the person I was meeting with had a lot of influence over my future. When my children were young, I taught them a calming exercise using a tapping technique: They would give themselves a butterfly hug while repeating, "I am calm, I am strong." I instinctively found myself sitting on the floor in my living room—seeking an unshakable foundation—tapping each shoulder gently in turn, like a warm embrace. Words started tumbling out of my mouth: *I am a loving mama. I am a good priest. I am beloved.* All of my anxiety dissipated. What was born that day was something I now call a Truth-Telling exercise.

When you find yourself anxious about the outcome of a brave conversation or a big life event, ground your body and find the words that are true now (before the hard thing), will be true while it's happening, and will continue to be true even if your big fears are realized. In other words, what are the truths about you that cannot be taken away? Here's a free one that you can always draw upon: *I am a beloved child of God.*

Awe: Goodness in Others

Occasionally I have an experience that restores my faith in humanity. It usually involves strangers coming together to help one another. I'm a sucker for the story of the soccer team gathering around their opponent when her hijab slipped off during play, so that she could replace it with

privacy. Or the grandma who forged an unlikely friendship with a young man she accidentally texted and invited
to Thanksgiving dinner, thinking it was her own grandson.
Awe researcher Dacher Keltner talks about the importance
of witnessing goodness in others. When we observe someone authentically caring about another, even in small gestures like walking an elder across the street, we are filled
with awe. This sense of awe is also activated when we read
about extraordinary individuals like Desmond Tutu or
Malala Yousafzai. Their words and examples inspire us. Take
time to notice the everyday gestures and the larger-than-life
models that remind us we belong to one another.

Retreat: Consuming

One Advent, my friend Megan and I led a retreat called
Holy Nourished. It was glorious: a house in the woods of
the majestic Pacific Northwest, and several souls gathered
to claim nourishment and rest. Megan and I had both experienced extreme approaches to wellness, but wanted something that incorporated soul care and focused on bite-sized
accessible practices. I taught tools for wholeheartedness, and
Megan guided us in the kitchen to create decadent meals
and adopt more intentional eating practices. What you consume on retreat matters, and I don't simply mean the food.
Many of us are accustomed to filling our brains with books,
social media, podcasts, TV, and more.

There's no right or wrong way to do this, but just like
with the Preparation spoke, I invite you to put thought and
intention into what you want to consume in your time set
apart. Perhaps you cook for others often and the thought of
having others cook for you or being able to dine out sounds
nourishing. Or maybe you don't often have the chance to

linger in the kitchen and cook at your own pace while dirtying all the dishes. Are there foods that are nothing short of divine for you, like a square of dark chocolate? Include that in your retreat! As for what you consume with your mind, ask yourself what you're missing—do you crave time to catch up on the podcasts or shows that never seem to fit into your daily life? Or are your days so filled with other people's thoughts that you need to turn all of that off and rest in your internal, holy wisdom?

Kinship: Seasons

Each winter, when everyone starts to grumble about it getting dark so early, I secretly revel in the shorter days. It's as if our earth—God's very own creation—reminds us that winter doesn't need to be a time when things ramp up or when we celebrate loudly. As the days fill with more and more beautiful darkness, we are reminded to slow our minds, to warm our bodies, and to find quietude in our souls.

What can we learn from the seasons through which we cycle? If you are a creature of habit, notice whether those habits shift at different times of the year. Scientists say that our bodies need up to two more hours of sleep in the winter. In January, you might feel a pull between the "new year, new you" resolutions, the annual meeting preparations, and the overwhelming fatigue that sets in after Christmas. I invite you to notice and honor the changes of the season and what they are saying to you.

A Prayer
for Enoughness

O Emmanuel, God with Us Always,
You came to earth to help us belong
and invite others into belonging.
Thank you for creating us in Your image.
May we speak gently
toward ourselves and one another.
May we choose to climb into the boat of empathy,
instead of simply waving from the shore.
May we embrace the wholeness of who we are,
and may that be enough.
Guide us to spread Your incarnate Love
to all whom we encounter
this day and forevermore,
Amen.

Being Vulnerable and Setting Boundaries

I sat there, quietly boring a hole through the candy dish with my eyes, wishing someone would offer me a piece of candy. I was eight or nine years old, a guest at someone's house, and no one ever did offer me that candy.

Why this takes up space in my store of memories, I'm not exactly sure. But I think it has something to do with speaking my needs into the world. A piece of candy may be inconsequential, but how can I expect someone to meet me in my need if I expect them to intuit my thoughts? How is it possible to get something if I don't even ask?

Have you ever wished, hoped, or prayed for something, but didn't tell anyone about it? I wonder how that worked out for you. I wonder what kept you from naming whatever it was you wanted or needed.

Asking for something from another is vulnerable. It might lead to rejection. It might lead to heartbreak. You might not be met with the affirmation you were seeking.

But what you don't always think about is the opposite taking place: how speaking your needs might improve your relationship, how it might open the pathway to love, how it might fulfill your dreams.

In this section, we'll look at the weariness around boundaries and asking for what we need. I'll introduce vulnerability and why we sometimes fear it, joyfully saying yes to that which is life-giving and no to that which is soul-sucking, and remembering that our belovedness isn't contingent upon how much we accomplish or what others think of us.

The Holy may know our needs before we ask (Matthew 6:8), but most of us don't possess that divine intuition. If there's something we long for, perhaps it's time to ask.

CHAPTER

6

Showing Up

[The magi] set out, and there, ahead of them, went the star that they had seen in the east, until it stopped over the place where the child was. When they saw that the star had stopped, they were overwhelmed with joy. On entering the house, they saw the child with Mary his mother, and they knelt down and paid him homage. Then, opening their treasure chests, they offered him gifts of gold, frankincense, and myrrh.

—*Matthew 2:9–11*

Have you ever walked up to a church building, only to find yourself face to face with a closed door?

One Sunday when I was in seminary, I visited a church for the first time. Navigating parking and finding the entrance to the building took longer than I anticipated, and I found myself walking up to the closed church doors a couple of minutes after the scheduled start time. Based on the orientation of the building, I wasn't sure whether opening the doors would place me at the very front of the sanctuary, the most terrifying place for a newcomer to walk in late. I was so nervous that I almost turned around and left. I don't even recall what happened next, only that feeling of wishing a hole would swallow me up.

Aside from being a cautionary tale of poor church signage and other things that keep visitors away, this story reminds me of how awkward it is to arrive somewhere for the first time, especially when you're arriving late. Some of my favorite latecomers are the magi, those persistent travelers who followed the star that rose the night of Jesus' birth, despite not knowing where it would take them. It's likely that their journey took them a few years, meaning they weren't even *fashionably* unpunctual to the baby shower.

Can you imagine showing up three years late to the party, not knowing if you're underdressed or brought the proper hostess gifts? Did this band of wayfarers have any anxiety about which door to knock on or whether they would have that door slammed in their faces?

I feel anxious when I place myself in the center of their star-following journey. I find myself curious about their persistence and bravery. I wonder how the magi knew they were bringing good gifts, or whether they boldly shared them not knowing what the reception would be.

What the magi practiced, and what I often cringe at, is vulnerability.

Vulnerability is, at its root, the risk of emotional exposure. And when we think of exposure, we might first think of being open to attack or hypothermia or a whole slew of negative things to which we could be exposed. But what about love? What about joy? What about fulfillment?

Here's the wild thing about vulnerability: Yes, if we open ourselves up, something terrible might happen to us. But also, something *wonderful* might happen to us.

To be vulnerable is to take a big risk, and those of us in vocations of service might find it tricky to balance modeling vulnerability, holding the vulnerability of others, and also keeping awareness of our unique leadership role and power differentials. In parish ministry, for example, I often experienced others being deeply vulnerable with me but didn't always feel able to reciprocate. They could tell me about their woes with a coworker, but I wouldn't share mine, since my coworker was also likely a pastoral presence to them. There was also the dynamic of wanting to hold space for their sorrow and grief without them feeling the need to hold space for my sorrow and grief. At the end of the day, though we shared in the same community, I always felt like I was primarily there to serve them. A relationship like this, which is—by necessity—unbalanced, doesn't make space for true mutuality when it comes to vulnerability.

There's another important ingredient to vulnerability: trust. A beautiful, albeit complex, dance takes place between trust and vulnerability: To be vulnerable with one another, we must trust one another, but the path to building trust is through vulnerability. So we practice sharing what I call *vulnerability nuggets*: small acts of vulnerability that build over time, based on whether they're met with empathy or solidarity. We share our story in small pieces that add up.

Vulnerability is a cornerstone of healthy relationships and communities. Allowing ourselves to go deeper with one another benefits the whole. In a society where we often exist and operate at the surface, it is important to have spaces to go deep and share our fears and our dreams.

I've watched many community members navigate the risks of abiding in love alongside one another. Particularly in the Church, some people attend simply because they might be seeking a quiet place to be alone with God or may be drawn in by the beautiful space and music. They may have no intention of loving or being loved. But then they open themselves up to relationship. They get to know the person in the pew next to them after the service, they work alongside a parishioner on a committee, their kids play together on the playground. And their heart aches when one of those people goes off to college, or finds a new job across the country, or becomes seriously ill, or dies.

It might be tempting to not open yourself up to love at all, to protect your heart, to engage only in minimal conversation to avoid getting too close. Love is risky; it will inevitably include loss and sadness. But it will also include great beauty. I have companioned folks in the deepest, darkest pits of crisis and grief; I have also blessed their newborn babies, shared wonderful memories of beloveds who have died, watched them find love again, rejoiced after successful surgeries, and joined their hands in marriage. Because in the world of God's love, we abide.

We remain wherever it is we're needed, whether it's pulling up a chair to sit with one another in the pit or jumping jubilantly to share in someone's joy. The more we let one another into our lives, the more we let God into our lives, and the more our love grows so that we may share it with all whom we meet. That's vulnerability.

Even if we can agree on the goodness of vulnerability, where are the spaces in which leaders can truly open our hearts, step into uncertainty, and embrace authenticity?

Vulnerability is not weakness, but rather is something that takes great strength and draws you into deeper relationship with yourself, one another, and God. As Brené Brown says, "Vulnerability sounds like truth and feels like courage." However, we all have masks and armor to protect us from being vulnerable, because while vulnerability is the first thing we seek when forming a relationship with another person, it's the last thing we want them to see in us. Facing our vulnerability opens the possibility that we are not enough. So we arm ourselves. We mitigate risk by shutting out vulnerability.

If you're serving in a setting where you feel constantly watched or judged, your vulnerability will only feel more unsafe. When I'm feeling vulnerable and don't want to be, I find myself acting in unhealthy ways like focusing on controlling my appearance or getting stuck in perfectionism.

When my coaching clients are preparing for job interviews, they're often trying to strike a balance between protecting their heart from falling in love with the job, town, or people—which could lead to getting hurt—and coming across as engaged and interested rather than distant. When you're trying to strike the right balance of vulnerability, you can work toward opening your heart while still claiming your boundaries. You can name what is needed to help you feel safe and what you hope to get from an experience. Even in the presence of a power differential, you can set your terms for vulnerability and thus establish needed trust.

Perhaps the clearest example of vulnerability and trust is a dog showing their belly. Their underside is soft and tender and not something they would expose if they're feeling threatened. But when they feel safe, belly up they go.

Reflection Questions

Consider a time when you felt like turning back at a closed door. What motivated you to press on, and what was the outcome?

Vulnerability involves risk but also opens us to joy and fulfillment. How do you navigate the tension between protecting yourself and being open to the potential of wonderful outcomes?

CHAPTER

7

Just Say No

> We cannot live in a world that is not our own, in a world that
> is interpreted for us by others. An interpreted world is not a
> home. Part of the terror is to take back our own listening, to
> use our own voice, to see our own light.
>
> —*Hildegard of Bingen*

"I'd rather walk my pet python," I declared proudly. When I was in third grade, my school sent home a list of phrases we could practice for saying no to drugs, things like: "No thanks, I prefer milk." I remember sitting at the dinner table with my beloved stepparent Dave, role-playing these scenarios. Thirty years later, I still remember our favorite: I'd rather walk my pet python.

There are many times when I wish I still had a list of practiced phrases to get me out of certain situations—social invitations, conversations with over-sharers, or an opportunity that looks good on paper but doesn't fill me with joy. I've spent time with my coaching clients, coming up with a similar list catered to them, and doing just what I did in grade school long ago: practicing saying no.

For the past few years, I've been asking what I call the Scandalous Question to folks in ministry. At first, I found myself whispering it, even if I was alone with one other person: What would it look like for you to say yes to more of the things you love in your ministry/job/vocation, and *say no* to the ones that simply don't give you life or complement your gifts?

It's scandalous because we're taught not to question or push back against the things we don't like or at which we feel inadequate in our jobs. To wonder aloud about a new way of living into our vocation might invite disapproval from seasoned practitioners or our own inner critics, and perhaps judgments that we aren't well-suited for our roles.

I think it's valuable to ask the Scandalous Question anyway! It's valuable because we're each equipped with a myriad of gifts, but no one person holds the same passions and skill sets as another. I often say that if we were all created with the same gifts, this world would be an incredibly inefficient and boring place. Each tax season, I gladly hand off my tax documents to a CPA. Am I capable of doing my own taxes? Yes. Is it the best use of my time or the best plan for mitigating overwhelm? Most definitely not. On the other side, I imagine there are many CPAs out there who would be terrified to sit by the bedside of a dying stranger or engage in public speaking. Setting aside the things that aren't *our* gifts opens up the opportunity for someone else.

Another reason for asking the Scandalous Question is that on the other side of every no is a yes. What are we opening ourselves up to when we set something else aside? What spaciousness might we step into or rest might we claim or new passion might we discover?

Earlier this year, I was at the *Philadelphia Eleven* film premiere; this documentary follows the first women to be ordained priests in The Episcopal Church in 1974. Several of the priests ordained in 1974 and 1975 were present at the premiere and held a panel Q&A afterward. I asked the women if they had any sage advice on burnout for those of you for whom I am writing this book. They certainly did, and some of it is sprinkled throughout these pages. But it was the *unasked-for* advice that stuck with me the most. A woman came up to me after the panel and said, "I heard your question about burnout. I think what you're describing is just called being an adult." She associated maturity with doing things that are emotionally and physically burdensome. She's not alone in that assumption. My question is whether we need to accept the premise that doing things well will inevitably wear us down.

My caveat with the Scandalous Question is this: There's always laundry to be folded. There will always be tasks that aren't our favorite but are necessary. But are we putting way too many responsibilities into that category?

After graduating from seminary, I taught high school for a year. The learning curve was steep, I loved it more than I had imagined I would, and I was utterly exhausted.

Every afternoon in my classroom, I packed two or three bags to overflowing. They contained my gradebook, lesson plans, student portfolios, instructor texts, and more. When I walked in my front door each evening, I let my heavy bags drop to the floor with a thud. The next morning, I found them in the same exact spot and threw them over my shoulder, my bags completely untouched except for my newly packed lunch.

I had great intentions of grading those papers and writing those lesson plans each evening, but I simply didn't have the energy. That was work I completed on weekends. All I was doing by carrying those bags to and fro was giving myself a huge heaping of guilt . . . and back pain.

Several months in, I had a frank conversation. I told myself that I could keep up this ruse and feel awful, or I could admit the truth and cost myself a lot less burden.

So I laid down my bags. I stopped schlepping misaligned intentions back and forth every day. I leaned into true rest each evening.

Like perpetually snoozed alarms and incomplete items left on your to-do list for ages, sometimes you need to be frank with yourself. Sometimes you need to let something go to make space for growth or rest. When you aren't honest with yourself and others about your capacity, overwhelm waits in the wings, ready to swoop in.

Setting boundaries and asking for what we need go hand in hand. There have been many points in my life where I've hedged an ask, giving people an out before I had even spoken my request. I'd say things like, "I wonder if maybe it would be possible for you to help me out, if it isn't too much of a burden. No worries if not!" Unsurprisingly, I said these things when I was the one who had trouble saying no. As I've gotten better at setting my own boundaries, I've learned to trust that other people can set their own boundaries as well. This allows me to make a bold ask and then believe the other person when they respond with a gracious yes or no.

People with poor boundaries don't always receive boundaries well, nor do people who previously benefitted from our poor boundaries. Many of us are socialized to believe that when we set boundaries or ask for what we need, we might hurt other people's feelings. And yet, we're all served by modeling and respecting good boundaries.

Reflection Questions

What would it look like for you to say "yes" to things that align with your passions and "no" to those that don't? How might this change your ministry or personal life?

In what areas of your life are you feeling overwhelmed by "shoulds?" What is one thing you can say no to this week to make space for something that brings you joy or rest?

8

Belovedness

And a voice from the heavens said, "This is my [Child], the
Beloved, with whom I am well pleased."

—*Matthew 3:17*

N o matter how many times I hear the story of Jesus'
baptism, I become like a small child—eyes full of
awe and wonder—when I hear about the voice
coming forth from the heavens. During a recent Epiphanytide retreat, we recalled Jesus' baptism and the Divine
words from above declaring Jesus' belovedness. At the close
of our three days together, time during which we built trust
and shared vulnerably, I invited everyone to stand in a circle.
Each participant, in turn, had the option of declaring aloud
"I am Beloved" or "I am a Beloved Child of God." Some
shouted it, others whispered it, many said it through tears.
In response, the gathered group responded back to them,
"You are Beloved" or "You are a Beloved Child of God."
Claiming that title and having it affirmed by others was a
powerful experience, and there was a lot of emotion in the
room.

It's not enough to hear or preach the story of Jesus'
belovedness; we must also claim it ourselves. I often encounter people in their later decades who still struggle to accept
the premise that they are beloved. Throughout their lives,

they've been told or shown otherwise. Claiming our beloved-edness is a radical act!

After one of the retreats I led, I was deeply honored to read a participant's journal, where she wrote of her experience as an LGBTQ+ person in a religious space, having experienced a history of religious trauma:

> No pretending here, no scout's honor,
> "I'm not divorced. I'm not gay."
> I am divorced. I am gay.
> And, I am . . . welcome?
> Shoes off, Jack Johnson T-shirt, jeans,
> And the host.
> I am a beloved child of God?
> Here . . . among the pines, with the lake.
> Maybe elsewhere.
> Not at home. Not with those that brought me
> to this earth.
> But [here]? With Callie?
> With these beautiful women?
> I belong.

Your belovedness is powerful. Your belovedness is not conditional. It isn't dependent on how many good acts you complete, what your societal status is, or how well others agree with you. It doesn't require that you be of a particular gender, race, orientation, culture, or religion. Sometimes we confuse belovedness with likability, and we refrain from fully embracing the person God calls us to be.

Several years ago, I would have told you I was universally well-liked: someone who made parents happy when friends or dates brought me home, a teacher's pet, an eager assistant to bosses. But somewhere along the way, I started speaking up more and earning a reputation as a troublemaker, especially when it came to issues of justice. I was genuinely confused at first, thinking people must have the wrong idea about me. And then I realized that my identity as a likable and agreeable person was no longer core to me, and that—even though I still really like it when people like me—it was more important to be authentic and stand up for what I believe in.

Despite how hard you might try to claim belovedness, it is important that you find spaces where you can be *shown* belovedness. You can read the words "you are beloved" ad nauseam, but it takes others reflecting your belovedness back toward you for it to truly sink in. It can't be just any person telling you you're beloved, however. It needs to be within a relationship where vulnerability and trust are present. Believing our belovedness requires vulnerability because we believe that we are beloved when others show up for us and truly see us. And we get to that place in a relationship by allowing ourselves to be vulnerable, to risk *being loved*. It doesn't require the perfect words or actions, rather a willingness to be messy and authentic with one another.

Believing our belovedness required trust because it's intimate. A pastor friend of mine shared the story of a staff exercise in which they were instructed to partner up and tell one another "You are loved." She was paired with an abusive coworker and asked to stare into their eyes for three minutes, so what could have been a beautiful experience was actually quite painful. It's an honor to reflect the belovedness that we see in one another. Otherwise, it can feel empty or forced.

Our belovedness is simultaneously the most basic truth and the hardest thing to receive. If we are *all* beloved, sometimes that means looking in the mirror and facing the truth that belovedness includes *you*; sometimes it means looking at another person and facing the truth that belovedness includes *them*. But belovedness is divinely given and not something we or anyone else can take away. We can, however, choose to live into it and to model it for others.

What does this look like in ministry? From what sources should we derive our belovedness?

Resting in our belovedness is profound and transformative. Just as the heavens opened and God declared Jesus as the Beloved Child of God, so too can we embrace our own belovedness. The Epiphanytide retreat experience I shared serves as a poignant reminder that claiming our belovedness is not only a personal affirmation but also a communal act.

Throughout our lives, we will encounter many things that challenge this truth: Societal expectations, religious doctrines, and personal experiences can cast shadows on the radiant light of our inherent belovedness. It takes courage and vulnerability to stand in the circle and declare, "I am Beloved" or "I am a Beloved Child of God," as the retreat participants did. This act of self-affirmation, met with the resounding response of "You are Beloved," contains the power to heal wounds and restore a sense of identity and purpose.

Aside from radically claiming our own belovedness, we must work to cultivate safe and inclusive spaces where all people can fully embrace their belovedness. Spiritual leaders can create communities of radical acceptance, where people can encounter and internalize the truth of their belovedness. These spaces must be marked by vulnerability and trust, allowing people to see and be seen in their entirety. There's something incarnate in belovedness: We can preach and model it even before we fully claim it for ourselves, because in doing so we are transformed. Telling others they are loved just as they are reminds us that we, too, are loved just as we are. In that truth, we will be set free.

Reflection Questions

How do you reconcile moments of feeling unliked or challenged in your beliefs with the deeper truth of your inherent belovedness?

Can you think of a time when someone mirrored back to you your belovedness? How did that experience impact your ministry and sense of self?

Part 3
SPARK Practice

nurture my **S**oma
engage in **P**reparation
make space for **A**we
claim **R**etreat
ground myself in **K**inship

Soma: Handle with Care

Do you sometimes feel like you're stretched so thin that an unexpected bump could completely pull you apart? You are most certainly not alone. I find that when I'm in a Season of Rough, I learn to bundle myself more carefully as protection against the elements of life. But when I've been experiencing a Season of Enough, I let my worn calluses soften and I'm not as prepared when the hard stuff hits.

A friend once shared a note their kid's teacher sent home from school:

> If your child is experiencing any sort of difficulty at home, I would like to provide additional support at school. I understand that you are not always able to share details, and that's okay. If your child is coming to school after a difficult night, morning, or week-end, please email me with the subject line "Handle with Care." No questions will be asked. This will

help me know that your child may need extra time, patience, or help during the day.

Imagine what it would look like if we all could wear little tags that read "handle with care" on days we needed a little bit more tenderness, compassion, and understanding. What practices do you want to put in place to ask for what you need? How do you want to be met when you're feeling tender?

Here are some ways you can use this concept with:

- beloveds: come up with a phrase to ask for gentleness (e.g., *I'm feeling tender today* or *I'm like a bruised banana*)
- coworkers or parishioners: share your needs without needing to share details (e.g., *I'm walking a loved one through a crisis right now and appreciate your understanding when I take longer than usual to respond*)
- strangers: no one needs to know what you're going through right now, but if you're in a situation that feels too much, feel free to excuse yourself or reschedule an encounter (e.g., *I'm holding a lot and need to postpone until I can be fully present*)

Preparation: Permission Slips

Whether you're new to claiming boundaries or it's old hat, it can help to have some supportive tools in place. My favorite tool—learned from none other than Brené Brown—is a *permission slip*. This is something we either give ourselves or ask for from a beloved to help us show up wholeheartedly. During some retreats, my participants will write a note giving themselves permission to not have to be the expert, to express their emotions as they arise, to take breaks as needed, or to turn off their phones to be fully present. Sometimes

I need permission from a loved one to take the afternoon off after a busy week or to preach a good enough sermon instead of a masterpiece (ironically, the former are often the ones that connect most with people's lives).

Having practiced phrases in your back pocket can also be helpful. When someone says "call me" without further information (cue panic attack) or requests a meeting, you can say: *Can you let me know the topic so I can best prepare?* If someone pops in your office for an unannounced visit, you can protect your time by saying: *I have 15 minutes now; if you think this might need more time, let's put something on the calendar.* When someone springs a question on a busy Sunday morning, you might ask: *Will you please follow up with an email so that I don't forget what we talked about today by the time I return to the office?* Setting expectations can benefit all parties.

Awe: Wonder Walks and Awe Ambles

I have a distinct memory of crawling into the root system of a tree when I was a kid hiking with my parents. It was not nearly so large or impressive as a redwood, but it swallowed me up nonetheless, and I felt held. One way to incorporate awe into your day-to-day practice is to embark on a wonder walk. (Depending on your mobility, this might be an awe roll or a wonder drive.) A wonder walk or awe amble doesn't necessarily have an agenda other than to move slowly and with great curiosity.

When I go on wonder walks, I welcome distractions. A fallen ice cream cone makes me send empathy toward the kid who has lost their sweet treat, a snail causes me to pause and consider its journey, a new bud on a tree reminds me to come back in a few days to witness the growth process.

Choose a route you've never been on to maximize your curiosity and awe. It will open your eyes to things you've never noticed before and recall your place in God's vast and wondrous creation.

Retreat: Digital Sabbath

I like to choose an anchor word at the beginning of each calendar year, as well as an intention word for each Lenten season. One January, the word *analog* came to me clearly. Analog, as in not digital. While I deeply love digital spaces, I knew that I needed to seek more experiences where I was offline. This manifested in a variety of ways, but one of my favorites was through listening to more vinyl.

We are a people who are deeply connected to the world through technology, and simultaneously isolated. Sometimes our devices remind us of the stress of work or keep us from true rest. I invite you to find periods of time to go offline. Perhaps you can set your phone to Do Not Disturb, have a device basket during mealtimes, go to a cabin without Wi-Fi, or engage in a social media fast. Which of those calls out to you most? Which feels the most challenging? By choosing to put parameters around our digital availability, we are claiming healthy boundaries and choosing connection.

Kinship: Vulnerability Tools

When we decide to be in relationship with one another, we are engaging in an act of vulnerability. But vulnerability doesn't always feel amazing. As humans, we will sometimes step on each other's toes, experience hurt, and wonder where we stand with one another. One of my favorite phrases for one of my least favorite feelings is *vulnerability hangover*. This is the feeling we have in the waiting period after sending a bold email, posting a major life change on social media, initiating a brave conversation, or sharing our feelings for someone. As I came toward the end of writing this book, I struggled to finish the last few hundred words. I couldn't figure out why, until my friend Jo said, "Then your book will be finished." That was the point all along, wasn't it? Except finishing the book meant that it would move on to editing, publication, and being shared with the world. And that's one giant vulnerability hangover.

Here are some of the tools I've found most helpful when experiencing a vulnerability hangover. The first tool is checking your story. I would guess that all of us have hopped aboard the imagination train and ridden it all the way to the station, any time we assume a lack of response or non-verbal expression means something terrible. Rather than letting that story guide you, check in with someone. You can simply say, "I haven't heard back from you and I'm making up a story that I put our friendship in jeopardy." Often, the other person will reassure you that it's an untrue story; in the rare case where it's true, you have an opportunity to repair the relationship. The second tool is related to the first: Sometimes you will say or do something you truly regret. You are a human being. Rather than building a house on a secluded mountain and resolving to live there the rest of your days, you can reach out to a friend and apologize, write a follow-up post on social media, or otherwise resolve the matter. Contrary to what your fears tell you, the sooner the better (but even if fear has kept you quiet for a while, there's still time to come back around).

A Prayer
for Saying No

O Creator of the Stars of Night,
how magnificent is that epiphany star
that points to the gifts that await us
and leads us onward toward our dreams.
May our "nos" be met with respect
and make room for faithful "yeses."
Teach us the dance of vulnerability and trust,
that we might boldly ask for our needs
and grow in relationship with one another.
On days when we feel weak,
hold us in our belovedness
and handle us with care.
In Your guiding name we pray,
Amen.

PART

4

Traveling Alone, Traveling with Others

M any of us fear loneliness. We also want to avoid the shame of comparison that can sometimes be activated in community. We might face the temptation to go it alone or the temptation to rely too heavily on others instead of drawing on our own strength. There are times in our journey when we're meant to travel solo and times in our journey when we're meant to travel with companions. Both of those can be beautiful, but we become weary when traveling alone leads to loneliness or traveling with others leads to unexpected isolation.

Several years ago, the wilderness summoned me. I told my spiritual director, "I need to go be in the wilderness, where all is quiet except for God's voice and my own." In my head was the advice of well-meaning friends, the needs of my beloveds which were at odds with my own needs, and the worry of what everyone else might think.

In this section, we'll wander alongside Jesus on his journey, beginning in the desert. We'll discover the gifts of the wilderness, including the nourishment we find in time on our own. We'll also look at how living with others means facing our own shame and cultivating shame resiliency. Finally, we'll remember that we were created to companion and be companioned along the way.

9

Wilderness Wandering

The wilderness holds answers to more questions than we have yet learned to ask.

—Nancy Newhall

Defining wilderness is a lot like traversing wilderness; it takes time, keen observation, and everyone does it differently. In 2020, when all gatherings moved onto Zoom because of COVID and I started leading online workshops and retreats, I fixated on the word *wilderness* because it felt so appropriate for the space we were navigating. In Christian circles, many faith communities had ceased worshipping in the middle of Lent, a liturgical season characterized by Jesus' wandering in the desert for forty days and forty nights. Even when Easter arrived, many of us still felt lost in the wilderness.

There are times when we're walking in a shared wilderness—natural disaster, global crisis, national tragedy—while also navigating our personal wildernesses. What I began to realize as I worked with more individuals and groups using the wilderness metaphor, was that we each picture different settings and conjure up different emotions when we think of the wilderness. For some, wilderness is the embodiment of fear and uncertainty, loneliness, and finding our way without a compass or map. For others, wilderness means adventure, discovery, and time alone with oneself and the Holy. I've been astounded at the range of definitions I've heard from folks. Wilderness is neither inherently good nor inherently bad. Some describe the wilderness as a deserted wasteland that lacks any landmarks for miles and miles, while others paint a picture of a forest so dense you can't see your own hand in front of your face.

I imagine that in his days of wandering the desert, Jesus found the wilderness, at turns, a place to deeply encounter God, face temptations, learn new skills, feel afraid, or simply wander.

In periods of wilderness wandering, my energy and creativity shift, sometimes in ways that I welcome and often in ways that frustrate me. I don't always have the inspiration or focus for writing that I want or need. And while I regularly guide the people I coach and companion to find compassion for themselves, I'm not always great about taking my own advice.

Here are a few things I know to be true of the wilderness:

Breaks are important.
So are guideposts.
The wilderness has many gifts to show us.

Breaks

I grew up near Chicago, one of the flattest places in the United States. So when I travel to places with high altitude, I tend to struggle. I recall a particularly challenging hike in Colorado. We'd only been in Denver for a day and a half, and my body was still adjusting to the altitude, but I wanted to climb a mountain. I wanted to take in the wholeness of God's creation. The entire hike was straight uphill, a 950-foot gain on top of the 5,000-foot elevation from which we started. My legs kept getting shaky from lack of oxygen, which is when I knew I needed a break.

Every five minutes, I had to find a rock to sit on or a tree to lean against in order to catch my breath. At home, I had been wandering in a season of wilderness—my own languishing and questioning my vocation—during which everything felt like an uphill climb for me. And unlike that mountain hike, there was very little opportunity to stop and rest or to catch my breath, though there were many times when I desperately needed a break.

In that wilderness season, some days I wondered whether I had what it would take to make it through. I hadn't yet reached the summit or seen the sights that would let me know that all is well. When we're on a long, arduous journey, we must take breaks. By continuing uphill with dwindling reserves, we're likely to fall. This applies to the wilderness seasons that feel exhausting as well as the wilderness seasons that feel exhilarating. What or who might be your sturdy rock to lean on as needed? How might we pause and catch our breath along the way?

Guideposts

I feel like I wander through the wilderness more often than not. Some of it I choose, and some of it is thrust upon me. I don't mind the wilderness. When I put myself in new situations or give myself space to dream, something transformative usually takes place.

In the wilderness seasons that are not of my choosing, I seek guideposts to find my way out; in the wildernesses I choose, I seek signs that tell me I'm on the right path and encourage me to keep going.

I often think back to a hike I took with my friend Sarah years ago in Arizona. We had put in a lot of work and felt good about the nature we had observed; we were ready to call it a day and begin the descent. But we encountered a couple of hikers coming downhill who said that the summit was just ahead and encouraged us to keep going. They told us that what was up there was worth it. And it truly was. Had we chosen to turn around sooner, there's so much awe and wonder we would have missed out on.

Other times, I'm looking for guideposts calling me to return. As we say on Ash Wednesday when imposing ashes and recalling our mortality, taken from God's words to Adam in the story of Creation, "Remember that you are dust, and to dust you shall return." God formed us, you and me, out of the dust. And God calls us always to return to the person God created us to be. One year my Lenten discipline wasn't fancy or complicated; it was simply the word "return": to return to self and to God. Through music, time with beloveds, walks in the woods, cups of tea, untimed cooking, books, knitting, meditation, and naps, I slowly found myself—and, ultimately, my way—once again.

Gifts

There are indeed many gifts to be found in the wilderness. There's a line from a Mary Oliver poem—"The Journey"— about leaving behind the shouts from others to mend their lives, and instead to journey until we begin to hear our own voice once more, "a new voice which you slowly recognized as your own, that kept you company as you strode deeper and deeper into the world."

At times, the only way to find ourselves is to get a bit lost. My dear friend Hillary, descended from the Chippewa people, has taught me to greet even the most terrifying of trails with a sense of curiosity and adventure.

Several years ago, I heard Brené Brown speak about her book on belonging, called *Braving the Wilderness*. She said, "There may be a time where someone says to you, 'You do not have what it takes to survive the wilderness.' And that's when you look inside your heart and then look them in the eye and say, 'Dude, I *am* the wilderness.'" In the wilderness, we discover a strength we might not have known we possessed. We spend time getting to know ourselves more deeply. And we learn what we truly need to survive.

When I lead folks through a wilderness exercise, I tell them about provision boxes that are posted along many wilderness trails, wherein you can leave behind the supplies you no longer need and pick up supplies from others that might serve you on the road ahead. As you wander seasons of wilderness, I wonder what it is that you've been carrying that no longer serves you. I wonder what you've picked up along the way that gives you strength. And I wonder what you might need for the journey ahead.

Reflection Questions

What "guideposts" have helped you navigate wilderness periods in your life? How have these influenced your journey?

The wilderness can offer many gifts. Reflect on a recent wilderness experience. What unexpected gifts did you encounter, and how have they enriched your life?

10

Lead Me Not
into Temptation

To receive this blessing,
all you have to do
is let your heart break.
Let it crack open.
Let it fall apart
so that you can see
its secret chambers,
the hidden spaces
where you have hesitated
to go.

*—Jan Richardson, excerpt from
"Rend Your Heart: A Blessing for Ash Wednesday"*

S everal years ago, I watched the following scene unfold on the internet: A few weeks before Christmas, someone posted a gorgeous photo of their church foyer in an online group for formation leaders. The scene appeared to be straight from C.S. Lewis' Narnia, with decorations and props adding to the ambience. They had created a space for church families to come and pick up materials for celebrating Advent and Christmas at home, during a time when churches couldn't meet due to the pandemic.

The post received many well-deserved accolades. Some were encouraged by it; others took it as an invitation to share the engaging scene and materials they had created for their own parishes. And then another post appeared. If social media posts could come across in a whisper, this one did. A brave soul at the back of the metaphorical class trepidatiously raised their hand and gulped and said, "Is there anyone else out there who hasn't had the time or energy or resources to create beautiful offerings for their congregations?" The comments rolled in. Everyone else who had been holding their breath said, "YES! Thank you! I don't have anything admirable to offer either. I'm trying to survive over here."

Both posts were a gift, the first one inspiring and an opportunity to share joy, the second honest and a chance to remember we're not alone. When we're wandering in the wilderness, many temptations beguile us. Not all of them are about power; many of them are rooted in shame, the belief that we are bad or less than. Shame crops up in many ways, luring us in with thoughts of scarcity or comparison, and reminding us to keep quiet lest others also begin to see our shortcomings.

Within that Christian formation group, I witnessed the ways in which comparison works in the digital space. We see something wonderful and may be in a place where we can celebrate it or be inspired by it, or instead we may be activated in our own areas of shame or not-enoughness (the feeling of being less than another).

In the digital spaces where we spend much of our time, life is curated. Even as someone who tries to model vulnerability and authenticity at all times, I get to choose what I put out in the world. I choose my photos, I choose my words, I choose whether to react or withhold reaction. We need the balance of digital space and physical space (both valid and beautiful in their own right) to grasp a fuller picture of how folks around us are living their lives. For every friend who shows up online with gorgeous hair and makeup, I need the chance to run into them at the coffee shop first thing in the morning and remember that they also wake up with bed-head and puffy eyes. For every tender anecdote shared about someone's marriage, I need to overhear the couple working through tension while trying to get through the security line at the airport. We are all human, and it's so helpful to remember that.

I sometimes forget the power I wield by having an online following; I recently got a piece of feedback that some people initially felt intimidated by me when seeing me on social media. My first reaction was to laugh, since I am very aware of my own shortcomings and certain that others can see those as well, followed by the thought that I never want to live my life in a way that makes others wish they had what I have. I'd rather live my life in a way that reminds others around me that they are so very loved.

What are scarcity and comparison and how do they impact our lives and our ministries? Scarcity is the belief that there's a limited amount of resources and not enough to go around. Comparison is to match ourselves against one another, which often leads to the belief that someone else is doing our thing but better. Both scarcity and comparison seem to reinforce that we aren't good enough, smart enough, attractive enough, wealthy enough, or successful enough, and that we're somehow deserving of our not-enoughness. This negative self-talk is rooted in shame, which immobilizes us or keeps us small. Instead of sharing our great gifts with the world (and we *all* have immense gifts), we keep them hidden. Sometimes this causes us to stay in toxic communities or abusive relationships, sell ourselves short, or inhibits us from following our dreams.

I've often heard that comparison is the thief of joy. I only recently realized it's not just our joy that's stolen as the one comparing ourselves to another, but also the joy of the person to whom we're comparing ourselves. This can breed resentment in relationships and diminish shared joy. We all thrive when we can partake in one another's joy and remember that there is no scarcity of joy to go around. Joy begets joy!

God calls each and every one of us to live into the fullness of life. We can strive to live into this fullness, not by following someone else's dream, but our own. The beautiful, unique iteration of humanity that only we can embrace. I was speaking at an event once, and afterward, a sixty-six-year-old woman came up to me and asked me for a hug. She had spent sixty-five of her years as a Roman Catholic, and seeing me—a priest, leader, mother, and woman—made her teary. I didn't dazzle her with my words; I simply showed up as me. Who *you* are truly matters.

As Jesus wandered through the desert, we know he faced temptations of grandeur, but I wonder if he also faced the temptation to reject the belovedness he had just been assured of in his baptism. I wonder if he doubted himself or contemplated living a solitary life to stay small.

Shame functions to isolate us from one another and keep us lonely. Being alone and feeling lonely are not mutually exclusive. There are times when we feel completely alone but not one bit lonely, and other times when we're in a crowd and yet feel completely isolated. According to the U.S. Surgeon General in 2023, loneliness and isolation have become an epidemic of our time. To push against it, we must begin to develop resilience to the things that draw us away from others and our own true selves. Shame never dissipates entirely, but what we can do is build up shame resilience.

The first key to becoming resilient to shame is recognizing when we're in shame. Through some of the somatic work we're doing in the SPARK Practice, we can become better connected to our bodies and aware of what they're trying to tell us. When I'm in a place of shame, for example, I can literally feel myself growing smaller. My shoulders come up around my ears, I lower my head, and I look away from anyone who's near me so that I don't have to meet their gaze. Another cue we're in a shame state is a shift in our self-talk. For me, I say things that are uncharacteristic; my self-doubt around things in which I typically feel confident skyrockets. I might even question my *persistent truths*, like "I am a Beloved Child of God" or "I am an excellent mama." Finally, many of us use the word *should* more often when we're in a place of shame. Shame presents differently in each person, but getting to know your signs will help you move to the next step.

The second key to shame resilience is to name our shame. We can do this by giving voice to our feelings of inadequacy and by sharing the stories we're making up. Silence can be like a petri dish in which our shame breeds and grows; shame tells us to keep our negative self-beliefs to ourselves because, otherwise, others will see us for who we truly are. Once we're in a place of shame the other shame starts piling on. If I miss a writing deadline, not only do I think of myself as an incompetent writer, but I start to wonder if I've been unfair to my family who has encouraged me in my writing and whether others can also see that I'm a failure. When I'm making up stories like this, the most effective thing I can do to stop the shame spiral is to text or call a beloved. I tell them I'm in a shame storm and let them speak truth into me or help me examine my untruths.

The third key to shame resilience is not to wander the wilderness alone. While there are certainly times we need to be on our own, we find flourishing when we are companioned by others.

Reflection Questions

What practices help you recognize when you're experiencing shame? How do you find your way back to self-compassion during those times?

How can you foster a community that supports shame resilience and encourages members to share their vulnerabilities?

11

Break Bread

When [Jesus] was at the table with them, he took bread, blessed and broke it, and gave it to them. Then their eyes were opened, and . . . [t]hey said to each other, "Were not our hearts burning within us while he was talking to us on the road, while he was opening the scriptures to us?"

—*Luke 24:30–32*

Here's something to know about me: I sometimes enjoy talking to strangers. My partner finds this absurd, especially when I do it while flying. I like making connections, particularly when we clearly have something in common. Have I approached people wearing clerical collars at the airport to excitedly exclaim, "I'm clergy too!"? Yes, I have. Do I stop to tell parents of wild children that their child brings me joy? Also yes. As for the flight itself, there are plenty of times I prefer to stare out the window, sleep, or take advantage of that focused work time that comes in the air, but from time to time, I like to engage. Once, I was in a row with a nervous flyer. She admitted as much to my seatmate and me, and I laughingly offered that—as a priest—I could pray over her. The person sitting next to me said she was a professor of religion and that she could also contribute. And in that moment a dear friend was born. Not only did we discover that I was a camp counselor in college with a dear friend of hers, but we immediately shared a soul connection. My plane friend Meredith remains an in-the-flesh friend to this day. We often exchange early morning texts with photos of natural beauty, excerpts from poems, life wonderings, and Holy Spirit musings.

My encounter with Meredith opened me up to another plane conversation a few years later. This time, a young man and I talked about our lives and how we spend our days. I told him I companion people on their journeys—my preferred verb for the way in which I accompany folks on their path of life. He pointed out that companion comes from the Latin *com*, meaning with, and *pan*, meaning bread. In other words, to companion is to break bread with one another. My eyes lit up. As a priest, I break bread with strangers and beloveds each week during the Eucharist. Of course, that's what it meant to companion.

I don't simply want to lead or guide or direct others; I want to companion them. Conversely, I deeply long to *be* companioned. I don't always do a great job letting others companion me, and I've coached enough people to know that I'm not alone in that. Being companioned is vulnerable and requires trust. Being companioned might agitate our shame because it requires that we admit we need one another. But it also diminishes the power that shame has over us.

Jesus' ministry journey begins with his baptism and immediate retreat to the desert. Upon emerging, the first thing he does is seek out companions for the way. This is not a coincidence. I imagine Jesus' time alone brought clarity that he would need to gather others with whom he could break bread and spread the message of God's love.

Years ago, I watched the film *Into the Wild*, based on the true story of Christopher "Alex" McCandless, who went on an epic post-college adventure. In an attempt at self-discovery and distancing himself from the darkness of a difficult home life, Alex wandered the country, met many companions along the way, and lived off the fat of the land. For months, he prepared for his ultimate goal: a solo journey in the Alaskan wilderness. On his journey, Alex befriended an army vet named Ron, who told Alex, "I'm gonna miss you when you go [to Alaska]."

"I'll miss you too, Ron," Alex responded. "But you're wrong if you think the joy of life comes principally from human relationships. God's placed it all around us; it's in everything, in anything we can experience. People just need to change the way they look at those things." Alex arrived in Alaska and wandered alone for more than 100 days, living off small game, rice, and local plants and berries. His joy at encountering the world all by himself started to subside, and he began to experience loneliness. But he was unable to cross the river to find his way out, so Alex remained tethered to an abandoned bus that became his shelter.

Toward the end of Alex's journey—as he faced starvation and death—his journal entries were written with less and less strength. He wrote in his copy of *Dr. Zhivago*, "happiness only real when shared." Despite what he tried to convince himself about joy coming not principally from human relationship, Alex discovered the truth, though perhaps too late.

While it is deeply important for us to find our own voice and to learn to be alone at times, we truly need one another.

In a transitional period in my life, I was on a wellness retreat for clergy when I took a walk down to the ocean. I was looking for inspiration, for answers. Instead, I saw this sign: Do Not Swim Alone.

Here's something I know about myself: I am great at collaboration until I'm facing a problem. Somehow, in the moment of challenge, I think that I must be the only person in the world. I get lost in the *shoulds*: I shouldn't trouble someone else with my problems; I should be able to figure this out on my own; I should've started tackling this earlier.

I certainly wouldn't want people to think I don't have it all together 100% of the time. (Secret: I rarely ever have it all together!) So, I try coming up with a solution on my own. I try facing the rising panic all by myself.

But sometimes . . . sometimes . . . I remember to reach out to someone to help me think through the problem or just to acknowledge and affirm that what I'm feeling is normal. When God created humans, God did not create them in isolation, but with a partner, a companion. We were never meant to go through this life alone.

When I bring others into the conversation, when I allow others to see my struggle and show me empathy or help me find a way out, there's a release that happens in my heart. I remember that I don't have to hold it all.

I shared this story with my pastor friend Betsy, who admitted to me, "I absolutely do this thing in regular life: pulling away from others at the moment when I should be drawing close, and thinking I have to be the hero of the story or the solver of the problem! Somehow, when the situation gets big and hard, I feel like I have to be bigger and harder, instead of smaller and softer and more open to connection."

I often pride myself on standing tall, plowing through whatever needs to get done, and not needing the input or assistance of others. But I'm so frequently reminded that when I'm my most wholehearted, authentic, fully alive self, I seek collaboration and partnership and community. Because we're meant to do this big, messy, beautiful, heartbreaking life together.

Reflection Questions

Reflect on the people you "break bread" with, both literally and metaphorically. How do these interactions nourish your spirit?

In what situations are you most likely to attempt swimming alone rather than reaching out to others? What could help you reach out for companionship instead?

What does it mean for you to be a companion to others? How can you actively seek to "break bread" in new or deeper ways within your community?

Part 4
SPARK Practice

nurture my **S**oma
engage in **P**reparation
make space for **A**we
claim **R**etreat
ground myself in **K**inship

Soma: Emotional Release

Laughter and tears both offer great somatic and emotional catharsis. Both cause a somatic release and often serve as a connection point with others. They're also deeply biblical: Sarah laughed, Jesus wept. My beloved spiritual director once proclaimed that our tears are reminders of our own baptisms, the waters of the Holy flowing through us. How can you weep when the world is already flooded with tears? Our tears for ourselves do not negate the tears of others. When we cry, we join in the collective grief, over lives and loves lost and powers abused and illnesses spread and people devalued.

When I need to be met in melancholy, Johnny Cash does the trick. If it's laughter I'm seeking, I find a kid in my life and watch their take on the world. Come up with a few go-to recipes for cultivating laughter and for accompanying you in sadness. Are there movies, music playlists, or nourishing foods that usher in this kind of release?

Preparation: Mindfulness

There will always be open tabs in my internet browser. I'm often dreaming up several personal and professional projects at once and not wanting to lose track of what I'm working on. My brain also has a lot of tabs open at any given time. I bounce between ideas and remember something else that needs to be done. Frankly, it's a bit overwhelming. When I have open tabs, my soul cannot fully rest. It's like a blinking light somewhere in the house, keeping me from falling into a restful sleep.

By engaging in mindfulness—that practice of being present to the current moment, including our surroundings and emotions, without needing to solve, ruminate, or judge—we can reduce our stress and increase our well-being. I like to do this through activities that require uni-tasking rather than multitasking. It might be through painting, cooking, refinishing furniture, or mowing the lawn. Anything that requires our full attention can help us slow down and be present. There's a lot we miss if we're trying to catch it all.

How might you engage in mindfulness in your daily life? Perhaps you can close your literal tabs each evening or give your full attention to the task at hand, in order to give your mind, body, and spirit the deep restoration it craves.

Awe: Art

When I was younger, I had a tenuous relationship with art museums. I thought there was a correct way to engage with them. If the person I was with spent a long time in a gallery that I didn't find that interesting, I thought I was doing it wrong. Then one day I went to the Art Institute in Chicago by myself, and a whole new world opened to me: experiencing art as I wanted/needed to experience it. I strolled briskly through some galleries and spent countless time in front of other pieces. I learned about what I appreciated in art and what I gravitated toward.

Through textile artist Mollie Donihe, I was introduced to the spiritual practice of *visio divina*—divine seeing or holy sight. In visio divina, you choose, or are given, an image to anchor you as you consider where the Holy is showing up or issuing you an invitation through the art. It works well for people who struggle with silent meditation because of a wandering mind. Visio divina can be done in an art museum, at home, alone or in community, with religious art or abstract images.

Retreat: Build Your Own

Give me a cabin in the woods with a kitchen and a beautiful view, and I'm as happy as a clam. When I tell others about that vision, I find people who deeply desire the same and people who think that sounds boring and awful. Going on retreat is a deeply personal experience that has to match your needs and personality.

Here are some questions to ask yourself when building your own retreat:

- Do I prefer complete solitude (cabin rental) or time near others (retreat center)?
- Would I like to come up with my own plan for my retreat (self-guided) or have someone else lead me (companioned)?
- Do I want to steep myself in prayer (monastery/convent) or practice (group retreat that focuses on a speaker or activity like yoga)?

- Would I prefer to cook my own meals (kitchen available) or have meals provided (hosted retreat/bed-and-breakfast)?
- What is my purpose for retreat? Rest and nourishment? Discernment and visioning? Connection and community? Production (e.g., a writing retreat)?

Not all retreats are created equal, so spend time thinking about what you need, and choose your own adventure.

Kinship: Celebrating with One Another

You may have heard of *schadenfreude*—finding joy in another's suffering—but do you know about *freudenfreude*—finding joy in another's joy? It's one of my new favorite practices, because it pushes back against the inclination to compare ourselves to one another or to fall into the belief that there's only so much joy to go around. Just as it's important for us to have spaces where we can express grief and disappointment, it's important for us to have spaces where we can claim our joy and celebrate with others. That's where we encounter the Holy. You can begin the practice by inviting others to share their joys with you, and then sharing your own as well.

A related practice is capitalizing on positive events, a research-based method of connecting with one another over the good things happening in our lives rather than gossip or complaining. It only takes five minutes, but the impact is long-lasting.

A Prayer
for Wandering

O God of the Wilderness,
help us to find gifts in this space—
solitude, courage, and self-knowing—
while giving us space to grieve
what has been lost and felt uncertain.
Guide us toward signs that You are always near,
and help us emerge changed for the better.
May we seek out sibling travelers for the journey,
choosing companionship and not comparison.
Let us break bread together
and know that Jesus is at hand,
today, tomorrow, and till the end of our days,
Amen.

PART

5

Recognizing Burnout and Overwhelm

I was in second grade when family friends visited Germany and brought back a piece of the recently crumbled Berlin Wall. I took the rock to school for show and tell, feeling excited by this piece of history that I didn't even fully understand. But after showing it off to my class, it ended up like many second-grade possessions: taking up residence in the bottom of my backpack. When I found it, weeks later, the Ziplock bag contained not one but multiple pieces of crumbled rock. I was so sure that I would get in trouble for being careless that I tried to hide the evidence, carefully super-gluing the pieces back together.

There have been many times in my life when I thought it was up to me to cover up the brokenness. I tried for years to curate happiness. Divorced parents, a toxic job, a failed marriage, a dead parent. I carried the hard stuff all alone. I held my own brokenness and the brokenness of others.

Over time, I've learned to follow my own truth. I've begun to believe in my belovedness. I've worked hard to draw boundaries and practice brave conversations. Thousands of people look to me as one who models vulnerability and authenticity. I preach a gospel predicated on brokenness and call it beautiful.

More than once, I've had to ask myself, "Why am I still trying to glue a piece of the Berlin Wall back together?"

In this section, we'll explore how embracing brokenness might lead to healing in ways that holding tightly to an illusion of wholeness cannot. When you find yourself walking through the valley of the shadow of death, sometimes you'll need to pause and stare into the tomb to know that there's life on the other side.

12

(Beauty in the) Brokenness

I wear my heart on my sleeve,
or rather both sleeves, since
it's usually broken.
Sometimes when I join my hands
to pray, the jagged edges
briefly touch,
like a plate that fell and cracked
apart from being asked
to hold too much.

—*"Second Helpings" by John Brehm*

I grew up in the Midwest, land of cornfields and soybeans. In college, I would frequently drive the two-hour stretch from my home in the densely populated Chicago suburbs to my college town in central Illinois. In between was a whole lot of nothing. And yet, my eyes would always find something to fixate on to keep me alert. My favorite subjects were old, broken-down farmhouses, ones that were leaning with age or which had sunlight streaming through the missing boards.

I've always been drawn in by that which is broken. Brokenness tells an important story.

In Japanese art, there's a practice called *kintsugi*, where they use gold lacquer to repair broken pottery, amplifying the cracks. The philosophy is that which is broken is part of the object's story and not something to cover up. The object's brokenness is worth highlighting.

Sometimes, moments of fracture are moments to stop and consider whether the way things were put together was indeed the best possible way. Let me be clear: God does *not* break you to make you stronger. But just like re-breaking a bone can get it to set properly, sometimes a thing—relationship, identity, belief system—that was broken can bring new healing and strength that wasn't possible while the thing was intact.

In the first half of this book, we've explored several sources of weariness that lead to burnout—feelings of loneliness and isolation, voices of shame that keep us from reaching out for help, and the belief that we need to do all and be all to everyone and everything. In the remaining sections, I'll guide you through not just overcoming burnout but developing more capacity to keep it at bay by prioritizing your rest, finding your purpose, and engaging your creativity. But before we move on, we must pause and peer into the tomb.

Assessment: How Dire Is It?

People throw around terms like stress, overwhelm, and burnout as if they're synonymous. While there is plenty of overlap, there are some important distinctions. Just like the relief you might feel in having a medical diagnosis after experiencing mystery symptoms, the right language for what state you're in can help you get the correct support and treatment.

In *Atlas of the Heart*, Brené Brown draws on the helpful story of a restaurant server to illustrate the difference between stress and overwhelm. In the restaurant industry, when someone is having trouble keeping up with their tables, they might come back into the kitchen and tell their coworkers, "I'm in the weeds." Others will jump in to help, and they'll call out needs: *Table 2 needs refills, order up for Table 6!*

If, however, a server comes into the kitchen and says, "I'm blown," things are a lot more serious. The kitchen manager will likely step in, tell that server to walk away entirely for fifteen minutes, and reassign their tables.

I'm in the weeds is stress; *I'm blown* is overwhelm. In stress, you may feel frenzied or in over your head. Somatically, your heart rate might speed up and your breath become shallower. When you're in a state of overwhelm, you may have some of the same emotions and physiological signs as with stress, but you will be less likely to notice them and far less likely to be able to interpret them. Overwhelm stops us dead in our tracks; we become immobilized. People around you may ask what you need, and you won't be able to tell them, because overwhelm shuts down our executive functioning. While it may feel like you need to make some tough decisions, you are literally incapable of doing so. The only thing to do is to go offline.

Both stress and overwhelm require telling someone else you are in trouble. Let's normalize that. We cannot get the support we need without anyone else knowing we need support.

If you are in crisis or are having thoughts of self-harm or suicidal ideation, you are so very loved. Please seek professional help, tell a trusted friend or colleague, go to the nearest hospital, or use one of the many options available to you. In the United States or Canada, you can go to nami.org/help for a list of mental health resources through the National Alliance on Mental Illness (NAMI). If you are outside the United States, search "crisis resources near me" or "mental health resources near me."

Remember, you are not alone.

All the tools in this book can help with stress. And yes, a high level of stress is known to be harmful. But it's overwhelm and burnout that are the most dangerous. When you're in a state of stress, you may still have access to your tools and have the ability to respond and move through that stress.

Burnout is a sustained or frequent state of overwhelm, especially as it relates to the workplace. We get burnt out in our jobs, which of course has profound impacts on the other areas of our lives.

Pinpointing what state you're in can help you decide where to go next.

Since I was a young girl, the Maundy Thursday service has been my favorite liturgy. After the service ended, while everyone departed in silence and the lights were still dimmed low, I would make my way up to the hand-stitched kneelers closest to the bare altar. I would sit or kneel there, and often weep. I was grieving for Jesus, betrayed and handed over to death, but I was also grieving for the ways in which I had been betrayed or the death that I had witnessed. Holy Week is a time in the church year when we can truly be met in our grief, heartache, and burnout. There's permission to go and sit in the tomb for a while.

So often we try to look past the tomb, avoiding death and moving straight to the promise of new life. If you're deep in overwhelm, you might worry that others will judge you or that they'll try to remind you of everything you have to be grateful for in an attempt to "roll away the stone." What you might need instead is to have your frayed heart held or to feel met by someone who has been in the tomb and made it through.

I once had a clergy colleague mock a phrase that's often thrown around in ministry circles: self-care. He said it was overrated. I pushed back, saying that I thought self-care was critical because, without self-care, we're likely headed down a path toward burnout. He retorted, "Every time I've burnt out, it's led to transformation."

That kind of silver-lining thinking feels like both a symptom and a cause of burnout. Yes, burnout *will* likely lead to transformation. That doesn't mean we should embrace it or ignore the signs. When those signs are paired with the sources of weariness we've examined, burnout may not be something we can come back from. I am alarmed by the number of faith leaders in my circles who have had a major mental health crisis or died by suicide in recent years. Having walked with a beloved through it firsthand, I can say that some days, they felt like death was the only option. Some days, they felt broken beyond repair. They needed to be reminded that we're all broken and that there is great beauty to be found in the brokenness. If this resonates with you, please know that there is help; see the resources listed above.

If you're peering into the tomb of burnout, you are so very loved and you are never alone.

Reflection Questions

How can embracing our own brokenness contribute to healing and personal growth?

Reflect on a time when you recognized beauty in something
broken or imperfect in your own life.

13

Now and Not Yet

I said: What about my eyes?
He said: Keep them on the road.
I said: What about my passion?
He said: Keep it burning.
I said: What about my heart?
He said: Tell me what you hold inside it?
I said: Pain and sorrow.
He said: Stay with it. The wound is the place
where the Light enters you.

—Rumi

arly one morning, I woke to the kind of thunderstorm where the flashes of light and crashes of thunder were on top of one another. There was a constant rumble and light show, rather than the predictable gap between the flashes and the crashes. Having no time to recover, my senses were heightened, and I found it difficult to settle back into sleep. This is sometimes how life feels. The claps of thunder come one right after the other, whether it be global tragedy or personal tragedy (like death of a loved one, chronic illness, relationship woes, major stressors, and much more). Early in the COVID pandemic, I asked my therapist: Is there really more tragedy right now or is it just harder to deal with?

She said, "Tragedy hasn't been canceled. Everything else has been canceled—celebrations, weddings, graduations, vacations." There was no balance. All the hopeful and joyous stuff had been put on hold, but tragedy had not been canceled. In the Christian tradition of Holy Week, we remember Jesus' journey toward death. Many of the days in Holy Week carry a strong story. On Palm Sunday, we recall the line of spectators as Jesus paraded into Jerusalem, foretelling the growing unrest as he spread a message of radical love and equity. On Maundy Thursday, there's Jesus' betrayal by a dear friend, a final meal shared with beloveds, and retreat to the garden for prayer. Good Friday tells the story of Jesus' arrest and unjust trial and, ultimately, his final breaths on the cross.

Then there's Holy Saturday, a day marked in large part by *lack* of a story—the great In Between. The space where grief is raw and joy has been put on hold. Holy Saturday is truly liminal space, the time after Jesus has died on the cross and the time before Mary Magdalene has encountered the empty tomb.

I've always experienced a quiet lull on the morning of Holy Saturday, even when I was a busy parish priest. It's a time of now and not yet, a pause between sobs, a chance to reflect on the precipice between life and death. We know what's on the other side of this story: love conquering fear, life triumphing over death, and rest for the weary. But what if we didn't already know the story? What if we didn't yet know that Jesus rose from the dead? What would that change?

Most of our life is spent in a Holy Saturday space. Unlike Jesus' disciples, we know that new life lies just beyond the ridge, but many of us still choose to emotionally abide in the now and not yet of that day. Practically speaking, Holy Saturday is a day when church altar and flower guilds are beginning to decorate, when preachers are writing the resurrection sermons they couldn't wrap their heads around until Good Friday had passed, the acolytes and lectors practicing for the festal services, the musicians and choir warming up to belt out the stowed-away alleluias.

Many of us are not solidly in life or in death, but living in the in-between, the waiting, the unsettledness of grief and joy (and back again). There's a lot of vigil sitting and soul searching and heart waiting that happens there. God finds us there, whether our faces are shining brightly or covered in dust and tears.

Holy Saturday spaces can feel like holding our breath for an inordinate amount of time. They can be thrust upon us, or something we engage in of our own choosing.

You may take the resurrection as a given, but what about the other places in your life where you don't know what lies ahead? I think of moments when I wasn't certain where the waiting would lead: the moment I asked everyone I knew to storm the heavens with prayers that my beloved dying parent might stay here on this earth, the time waiting for the results of a breast biopsy as a young mother with a nursing infant, the countless times I accompanied dear ones through diagnoses, divorces, and deaths.

It is a deep honor to walk with others through the valley of the shadow of death. But in so doing, you must also make sure you have your own spaces to grieve. How can you choose Holy Saturday spaces, where no expectations are placed upon you but where you can immerse yourself in the wallowing and in the waiting?

These In-Between spaces are important and sacred.

Sitting with yourself in your grief is important and sacred.

Honoring the darkness of the tomb and the wisdom found there is important and sacred.

It is often in the darkness that I most richly encounter the Holy. The darkness is that which births: the formless void from which God creates; the womb. The darkness is where we go to feel safe: under the covers; our face buried deep in a hug. The darkness is where creativity dwells: the theatre; the vast expanse of interstellar space. The darkness is where we often encounter intimacy: closed eyes in prayer; the arms of our lover.

In this life, there's time for healing, time for rejoicing, and time to return. None of us can say for sure what tomorrow will bring. But in the space of Holy Saturday, I invite you to rest. Perhaps this is *not* a space where you're called into being joyful, productive, or radiant. Perhaps Holy Saturday spaces are for tenderness, quiet, and connection. The Holy is with you in the waiting. God sits in the space of grieving and worry, and God sits in the space of love and hope. Whatever you are awaiting, know that you are not waiting alone.

Reflection Questions

How does the story of Holy Saturday resonate with your experiences of being in between significant events or decisions in life?

In what ways do you encounter God in the darkness?

Part 5
SPARK Practice

nurture my **S**oma
engage in **P**reparation
make space for **A**we
claim **R**etreat
ground myself in **K**inship

Soma: Breath

I had a spiritual director named Mollie in college, and one day Mollie referred to the focused breath that one uses while running. As an asthmatic and an anxious young soul who had not yet learned the power of breath, I was bewildered. I had no idea what she was referring to. It would take several more years for me to gain greater awareness of my own breath and its importance in mitigating anxiety and stress. It turns out focused breath is key for everything from managing pain to increasing pleasure. My youngest is an empathetic soul and often suggests I take a deep breath when he senses me holding tension. He's onto something.

One tool for embodied breath is called Box Breathing: As you inhale, begin drawing a box in front of you with your finger. On the upward gesture, inhale to an internal count of four. Draw your finger across the top as you hold your breath, exhale on the down, and hold again across the bottom, all in counts of four. As you repeat this, you'll likely find that your anxiety dissipates, your body relaxes, and your thoughts clear.

To incorporate a spiritual practice into your breath, try a Breath Prayer: a simple repeated mantra on the inhale and exhale. I love drawing on the beautiful offerings of Cole Arthur Riley in *Black Liturgies*, or a mantra like, "[inhale] God of stillness, [exhale] bring me peace." You might even pause to notice where you're holding physical or emotional pain in your body and focus your breath prayer on that spot.

Preparation: Slow Start Mondays

One of my favorite ways to prepare for the week ahead is Slow Start Mondays. Since Sunday is often a workday for me, I like the chance to ease gently into my week, get in some movement and a nourishing breakfast after getting the kids off to school, and sit down with my planner and a cup of tea. I use this time to copy items from my digital calendar to my "paper" planner (I use a tablet and stylus), allowing me to pray over the week ahead and find gaps that I need to fill in with rest, soul tending, or long-range projects. I use four colored categories for my week—home, work, writing, and body and soul—to plot my items so I can easily see where there is imbalance.

This is also a great time to engage in a *drain/fill assessment* I first learned from my friend Jenn. There are things in our schedule that are energy drains (e.g., soul-sucking meetings) or fills (e.g., life-giving encounters). Take any week—one that has passed or the one coming up—and look through each item on your calendar, noting D for drain and F for fill. If your week contains far more drains than fills, what can you do to find equilibrium? Perhaps it's adding in a short walk or tea break between two drains, claiming extra rest that week, or delegating some of the drains. If one or more areas of your life are substantially soul-sucking, perhaps it's time to consider a bigger change.

Awe: Reverence

When my extended family gathers at the beach, there's usually a dash to dip our toes in the ocean upon arrival. On our last trip, the waves had white caps and there was a riptide warning for the first day and a half. Despite wanting to make the most of our time near the water, I was clear about waiting to go in. I felt, in equal parts, reverent and fearful of the ocean. She had spoken, and I respected this force that was so much greater than myself.

The words awesome and awful are both rooted in awe, that thing which inspires both fear and wonder. So much of nature can be simultaneously beautiful and dangerous—fires, blizzards, storms. Sometimes you will experience awe in the most unlikely places and in experiences that also cause fear. These are invitations to pause and reflect on the magnitude of creation.

Retreat: Toddler Day

In the midst of a season when I was running at an unsustainable pace, I headed to the mountains for a few days off the grid. It was there on a farm in the mountains that I met Margo the Pig. Margo was jovial and seemed quite content with her life. She certainly did not work straight through lunch or send "one last email" on her day off or scroll through her phone when her body was begging for sleep. Margo rolled around in the dirt to keep cool, made a point of greeting any human who came to say hello, and snorted excitedly when getting ear scratches or pieces of popcorn.

How can you live more like Margo the Pig, making time to truly listen to your body, be fully present to your loved ones, and prioritize delight and gratitude? Plan a Toddler Day. A day to let your most primal needs guide the way. Sleep when your body wants to sleep. Eat whatever your body craves whenever your body craves it. Watch favorite movies, listen to familiar music, wrap yourself in creature comforts.

I invite you to apply this idea of a toddler day to your at-home or overnight retreat. Pack or stock your space with a possibility bag—spiritual books and trashy novels, a fiber arts project, paper for reflecting, a coloring book, a meditation stool, and a comfy pillow. If the only thing you take out on your retreat is your pillow, you haven't failed. Listen to your body and live like Margo.

Kinship: Short-Form Connection

Human connection is an effective antidote to burnout, especially when it involves physical touch. Based on collected research on wellness and happiness, I'd like to introduce a menu of short but life-changing options: the twenty-second hug, the six-second kiss, and the eight-minute phone call. We have all heard that loneliness has reached epidemic levels and causes both mental and physical health issues. Each of these options has the benefit of decreasing stress and blood pressure and increasing your connection with others.

Studies have shown that a long hug (twenty seconds or more) multiple times a week has the biggest positive impact on health, so find yourself a consenting friend, partner, or pet; benefits are even shown from hugging yourself or a pillow! Similarly, relationship expert John Gottman makes a case for the six-second kiss. If you have a romantic partner, kissing for at least six seconds requires intentionality and is long enough to release oxytocin. Finally, I learned about the eight-minute phone call in the *New York Times* "7-Day Happiness Challenge." People often put off catching up with loved ones because they're too busy, but eight minutes is short enough to fit into your schedule and long enough to cover substantial ground. If you're lacking in the kinship area, text a friend and ask if they have eight minutes to catch up, honor each other's time, and plan another check-in soon.

A Prayer
for the Tomb

O Holy One of Refuge and Strength,
let our cry come to You.
We feel lost and helpless;
we feel stuck and overwhelmed;
we don't know where to turn.
From where shall our help come?
In our brokenness, may we find healing.
As we walk through the valley of the shadow of death,
may we not fear but feel Your presence.
Let us peer into the tomb and not be devoured.
Remind us of the Light to come.
In sorrow and trembling we pray,
Amen.

PART

6

Prioritizing Rest

When it comes to rest, I wonder if Jesus fell into some of the same traps that anyone in a service vocation falls into—the belief that we must show up for everyone all of the time, even when we have nothing left to give. There are many gospel stories in which Jesus tries to model good self-tending by taking a nap or withdrawing from the crowds. And yet, they always draw him back in.

It is deeply important to cultivate collaborators with whom to do work and life, and to learn how to say no in order to protect your boundaries. But it isn't always that you don't know how to say no. I bet if you were to be honest with yourself, you sometimes take pride in your weariness. You might wear your exhaustion like a well-earned badge. In this section, we'll learn how to have life beyond the tomb, how to begin seeking life again, and how to prioritize rest.

CHAPTER

14

Glimmers

"Woman, why are you weeping? Whom are you looking for?"

—*John 20:15*

"Why do you look for the living among the dead? He is not here but has risen."

—*Luke 24:5*

I consider car dancing one of the highest forms of unbridled joy and playfulness. You know, the person at the stoplight in the lane next to you who's drumming on their steering wheel and belting out lyrics to their favorite song. When I encounter a car dancer, my whole day is made better. And when that person is me, my heart soars and I feel completely free.

Throughout my life, the physical attribute people have commented on more than anything else is my smile. I smile easily and not in the "women are socialized to smile and be polite" sort of way. I genuinely enjoy life 95% of the time, and I love connecting to and encouraging others with a big ol' grin. So it's not insignificant that in one of my most difficult seasons, I forgot what my laugh sounded like. I felt like I was living underwater, where voices were garbled and everything appeared blurry. I deeply wanted to feel like myself once again.

I decided my guiding word for that leg of my journey would be *return*. I wanted to return to me, to find Callie again. I was worried that she was gone forever. But little by little, I found her. I found me. Each time I felt even slightly myself, I would pause and take a photo, write down what was happening in that moment, or simply utter the word "return." It was my own reminder to myself that I was in there. That my delight at the tiny-but-not-inconsequential things in life like crunchy leaves, a mug of my favorite tea, or fresh sheets on the bed wasn't gone forever. That my capacity for playfulness was still accessible. That new life was possible.

I didn't know there was a word for it at the time, but what I was seeking were *glimmers*. For many years, mental health professionals have used the word trigger to identify something that activates our anxiety or depression. A trigger is something that makes us feel unsafe or brings up grief, such as a friend's pregnancy announcement to someone experiencing infertility or unexpectedly seeing a photo of someone we've been hurt by.

But more recently, mental health professionals have started talking about the opposite of triggers as *glimmers*. Glimmers are as they sound: tiny but not inconsequential moments that remind us that we're safe and grounded and that joy is possible. Instead of our heart rate increasing like it does when we experience a trigger, glimmers cause our heart rate to slow and send our nervous system the message that we are okay. Each time I felt a piece of my essence returning, I was experiencing a glimmer shining through.

In the last section, you peered into the tomb of overwhelm and burnout. It is time to peer into the tomb again, but this time with the hope of finding something different. When

Mary Magdalene arrived at the tomb in John's gospel, on the third day after Jesus was laid to rest, she was deep in grief and was—understandably—expecting to be met by death. Instead, she found that the stone had been rolled away and there was no body lying within. Still, Mary didn't trust that someone hadn't stolen Jesus' body or that there wasn't some other explanation. When she encountered the risen Christ, initially thinking him to be the gardener, she heard the words, "Woman, why are you weeping? Whom are you looking for?" In Luke's account, Mary and the other women hear the words, "Why do you look for the living among the dead? He is not here but has risen."

What are you looking for? He is not here but has risen. How might we reorient ourselves toward looking for life after burnout and loss? How do we start seeking life again after we've learned to expect death?

It's a complete shift of our body, mind, and spirit to look for glimmers of life rather than signs of death. It might require you to retrain your brain; just as negative thinking begets more negative thinking, so too does positive thinking beget more positive thinking. In addition to actively cultivating a practice of seeking new life—through such tools as a gratitude journal or practice of the daily examen—you can also be ready to catch the signs of life when they spontaneously drop into your awareness.

I sometimes see a dozen clients a week, from all over the United States. It's a small sample size, but connecting with people from so many diverse climates and time zones allows me to notice patterns. It feels a lot like acting as a barometer. When it's raining hard here in Philadelphia, I'm amazed to sign on with one of my clients in Rhode Island or Washington, DC, and see it pouring outside their window as well.

When I encounter several people in a week who have a flu outbreak in their family, my casual observation is that cases are on the rise across the country. But I also observe patterns in our mood and state of mind, sometimes with seemingly no direct correlation to what's happening in the world. In some seasons, even in weary seasons, I've witnessed an uptick in flourishing.

It seems so strange, and it comes in unpredictable waves, but dreams find a way of breaking through seemingly perpetual crisis or strife. Perhaps it's like hope being born of struggle; in hard seasons, I encounter a plethora of people who are coming up with new ideas, finding a deeper meaning, or plotting to change the world for the better. I can't explain this in a scientific way except that goodness begets more goodness. Giving yourself permission to dream gives others permission to dream.

Music is a sign of reconnection with myself: I catch myself singing in the shower, or dancing in the kitchen with my partner or kids. When I'm dreaming, my body feels rested, my heart feels full, and my mind feels at ease. My inclination is to keep quiet when I'm experiencing new life, but this is what I've come to realize: I say it out loud to claim joy and to make space for dreaming in the midst of a world of nightmares. We are a resilient people. Our human arc is always bent toward hope. My therapist once showed me a line illustration of resilience: It isn't a flat line without change, but neither is it a mess of towering spikes and bottomless pits. Instead, resilience is a line that ebbs and flows like the ocean, changing as we experience joy or trauma. The highs gently bump against the top edge and the lows gently bounce off the bottom edge, always coming to catch their breath at home base in between.

Building resilience takes practice. It takes support. It takes vulnerability. We must claim the highs when they come so that we can weather the lows. We must dream the dreams so that we can survive the nightmares. We must live into the joy so that we can be present to those in pain. Like a flower growing through a crack in the concrete, life finds a way to persevere.

Reflection Questions

Think of the concept of "glimmers" and how recognizing small moments of joy can impact our well-being. When has a glimmer helped you through a tough time?

How can actively cultivating a practice of seeking resurrection change your outlook during difficult periods?

15

Give Rest to the Weary

Keep watch, dear Lord, with those who work, or watch, or weep this night, and give your angels charge over those who sleep. Tend the sick, Lord Christ; give rest to the weary, bless the dying, soothe the suffering, pity the afflicted, shield the joyous; and all for your love's sake. *Amen.*
—*The Book of Common Prayer*

The disciple Thomas is away when Jesus first appears to the other disciples after his resurrection. Thomas is quite understandably wary when his friends tell him they saw Jesus. Perhaps it was FOMO (fear of missing out) or maybe it was mistrust of his sibling disciples, but he wasn't inclined to simply take their word for it. When the time comes for Thomas to encounter Jesus in the flesh, he asks for *more*. It isn't enough for Thomas to hear Jesus' voice or witness him with his own eyes; he feels the need to touch Jesus. This act has earned Thomas the unfortunate moniker of Doubting Thomas throughout much of Christian history. However, I've encountered more people who share a deep affinity with Thomas and want to defend his reputation than those who deride him.

Earlier, I talked about practicing vulnerability and asking for what we need. Trust and vulnerability are a dance; in order to begin trusting someone, we must be able to be vulnerable around them, and in order to feel comfortable being vulnerable, we must first trust someone. That feels a bit discouraging, like we might never make any headway. But, there are ways to build trust and practice vulnerability simultaneously; it simply takes a little back and forth. You can test out how it feels to share something tender about yourself and wait to see if your tenderness is respected, met with empathy, or matched by the other person sharing something tender as well.

Thomas had presumably already built up trust and shown vulnerability with Jesus in their time traveling together, but trust and vulnerability often have to be established again and again. The dance continues. Part of the ongoing vulnerability is speaking up and asking for what we need, and part of continued trust-building is making space to meet the needs of others.

I wonder: What if Thomas wasn't filled with doubt, but longing for the authentic building of trust? What if he wasn't Doubting Thomas but Trusting Thomas?

In asking to touch Jesus' hand and side, Thomas was requesting intimacy, a deeper connection, an honoring of what he knew he needed. And one way we can read Jesus' response—*Blessed are those who have not seen and yet have come to believe* (John 20:29)—is that it must be even harder for those who cannot experience the assurance of trust firsthand.

What does trust have to do with rest? I am unlikely to engage in true rest without relationships of trust. I must listen to and trust my own body when it tells me it needs rest. I must also trust others around me to pick up any of the slack that I might leave by claiming rest (which also requires me to trust that they, too, will claim rest). And finally, I must trust that when someone grants me rest, they truly mean it.

I have a neurological disorder that impacts my sleep and has come with a lifetime of extreme fatigue. Somewhere in my childhood, I picked up the message that sleeping in is lazy. On the rare Saturday when I get to sleep in, I start to feel uneasy as soon as my family begins moving around in the kitchen. Even if they're having a grand time or planning on treating me to tea in bed and a slow morning, I feel like I must be letting someone down. I must specifically ask if I'm needed and trust my beloveds when they tell me it's okay to rest. It slowly chips away at my narrative that rest is bad or burdensome for others.

During the year I taught high school, I knew that I would need a space to take a short afternoon nap as a way of managing my fatigue. I was so embarrassed to make the ask, but I knew that making it through the school day without rest would be difficult. So I courageously asked for the rest I needed and worked with the administration to put a cot in a quiet, unused space.

There are so many barriers to claiming rest. Rest is elusive, especially when you aren't intentional about building it into the rhythm of your life. It's common to avoid rest, especially if you equate rest with laziness. Rest is complicated, even more so for those without the privilege of time or the freedom to claim rest without being judged for being slothful. When you have too much on your plate or can't quiet your mind, you're unlikely to be able to engage in true rest.

Without adequate rest, you may begin to lose grip on the things that matter most: your big dreams, time with your beloveds, the tools needed to be your best self. There are also deep physical and mental health impacts stemming from ongoing fatigue, such as short-term memory loss, delayed reaction times, and increased irritability.

Many of us conduct our lives as if exhaustion is a given. But what if it weren't?

In the United States, *grind culture* has become the norm. Grind culture is the idea that there's always more work to be done, and it glamorizes capitalistic thinking. Theologian Tricia Hersey—who calls herself the "Nap Bishop"—teaches that grind culture is rooted in slavery and white supremacy and most negatively impacts BIPOC individuals. Claiming rest is more difficult for those on the margins, due to overlapping issues like lack of workplace support, unrealistic societal expectations, and a deep history of treating Black and Brown bodies like machines rather than humans made *imago dei*. Hersey's work through The Nap Ministry paves the way for a new idea: *Rest is Resistance* (also the title of her book). Rest is resistance because it pushes against the hustle and grind and asserts that we are not meant to orient our lives around productivity and the tyranny of the urgent.

Rest is resistance because exhaustion has become a false idol for many of us. In Christianity, we strive to follow the counterculturalism that Jesus modeled. Even so, the Church is certainly not immune to grind culture and leaders often compare our busy schedules as a main topic of conversation. If we truly want to be countercultural, we'll begin not only teaching and preaching rest, but modeling it firsthand. You are enough, just as you are. Your worth is not bound up in your full calendar, and your value is not measured by how little you slept last night. To claim rest for ourselves is to claim rest for all. It's to say that all are created for rest and not for constantly making, doing, and striving.

The disciples who didn't need to touch Jesus weren't wrong. Thomas, needing a little extra assurance, wasn't wrong either. Claiming rest and asking for what we need is about listening to our own selves. Allowing shame and comparison to crop up only diminishes the possibility of living a life of flourishing. One Friday at sundown, the beginning of the period of sabbath for Jewish people, Rabbi Danya Ruttenberg posted: "In a culture that assigns value to people based on their productivity, it is a radical act to choose to rest. Your value is not in what you do or make." May you choose rest.

Reflection Questions

What role does trust play in allowing yourself to rest, and how can you build that trust within your relationships and communities?

Reflect on how grind culture impacts your life and how you can resist it to claim rest for yourself.

CHAPTER

16

Time Set Apart

I was passing by
My sister called me in
And she said to me
Why don't you take time in life?
'Cause you got a far ways to go

—Liberian folk song

I **aspire to be someone** who takes time in life, who is open to the chance encounter I never would have made if I were engaging in my usual hustle and bustle. As I was finishing this manuscript, I took myself on a solo writing retreat. It gave me the time I needed to have several focused writing sessions a day without being interrupted or tending to my beloveds (whom I adore and for whom I would drop anything). I stayed in a small fishing village and made my way around on foot. I realized that, in doing so, I didn't just create space for my writing, but also space to slow way down. If someone wanted to talk on my way to find dinner, I stopped and said hello and didn't come up with an excuse to walk away. The deep breaths I found myself taking were a reminder that this is my preferred pace of life.

There are times when we choose to engage in rest and times when rest chooses us. I think of this as a distinction between claimed rest and forced rest.

Claimed rest is rest we make time for. It might be a daily afternoon nap, a planned vacation, a social media sabbath, or a day off. I usually know that I need to make time for rest when I find myself fantasizing about it. One summer, shortly after moving into a new house, I kept finding myself dreaming about one hour in my backyard hammock. I thought I needed everything to align to make that possible: completed work tasks, entertained family members, a calm dog, temperate weather, and an unpacked house. I wanted to feel settled enough to justify taking that time for myself, a moment to regather and rest for the journey ahead. The afternoon I finally claimed my hammock time was imperfect, a fleeting moment between Zoom calls, and—inevitably—an injured child. But for two minutes I closed my eyes and soaked up the sunny bliss that was a moment of quiet. Rest is elusive and there's often a crisis erupting, but that doesn't mean we don't need a moment of claimed respite.

Forced rest can happen in a variety of ways. The one that many of you have likely experienced is the sickness that follows a big event or holiday season. Your body seems to say, "I've had enough; I'm going to make you slow down now." There's also the forced rest of an unexpected job loss, injury, or other life event that puts a big pause on life. This forced rest can feel like an unexpected gift or a giant burden. During my senior year of high school, I was in a major accident, hitting a tree while skiing with my parents. The timing wasn't great; I was less than three months from graduation. While there were many positives that came from that season, it wasn't the way I would have chosen rest for myself or my family. I don't recommend waiting for forced rest to find us in order to slow down; we can choose to make the best out of a season of unexpected rest, but the stress that accompanies it often cancels out the benefits.

There's a third category as well. I call it *half rest*. I have long prided myself as a person who models good rest: taking a period of sabbath each week, prioritizing my family above all else, and napping regularly as a way to stay healthy and focused. But sometimes what I engage in is actually half rest: a state somewhere between activity and passivity, that is neither productive nor restful. At the end of a long day, when I don't have any more energy, I often find myself scrolling through my phone in a mind-numbing review of social media. When I finally come to awareness, I realize that my soul wasn't fed, my body wasn't rested, and my laundry was certainly not folded. So I lose an hour of time that could have been constructive or restorative, but instead existed in the limbo of neither-not-yet-ness. One way to avoid half rest is to check in with yourself about what your body, mind, and soul most need. If it's rest, give yourself permission to fully lean into rest and be intentional about engaging in something life-giving: perhaps a bath, an episode of a favorite show, a leisurely walk, or a cup of tea.

God is not neutral about our rest. In fact, God commands us to take Sabbath, to rest from our labors, to set aside a period of time in which we are not producing or consuming, but simply being. Extravagant rest would be establishing a sacred weekly practice dedicated to this restoration of wholeness and resisting those practices that merely provide numbing or which become a priority above being in right relationship with God, ourselves, and one another.

In mindfulness, there's a concept of "non-doing." It's time that comes without an agenda, and it is one of the best responses to feeling burnt out or overwhelmed. You may recall that in overwhelm, you're immobilized and not capable of making decisions, so stopping everything is your best first course of action. At the beginning of my retreats, I often share this line: "Nothing is required of you in this space. You don't need to caretake or impress or give a book report afterward. Nothing is required of you." Across the room, tears begin to fall. So many areas of your life require that you meet goals or deadlines or have something to show for the time in which you've claimed rest. Sometimes you keep moving because you're afraid of what might happen if you pause: what feelings might arise, what truths you might have to confront. What would it look like to set all of that aside and sit for a moment? With yourself? With one another? Why don't you take time in life, 'cause you've got a far ways to go.

Reflection Questions

What is your understanding of "claimed rest" vs. "forced rest" in your own life, and how do each of these affect you differently?

How can we intentionally resist "half-rest" moments that lack true restoration? Where are you finding moments of rejuvenation in this season?

Part 6
SPARK Practice

nurture my **S**oma
engage in **P**reparation
make space for **A**we
claim **R**etreat
ground myself in **K**inship

Soma: Naps

I look forward all year to the Easter afternoon nap. There's nothing quite like a well-earned rest and no immediate to-do list on the other side of it. As someone prone to extreme fatigue, I am a nap evangelist. Some of us think that we need three hours, a darkened room, and four pillows for a sufficient nap. While that sounds lovely, a nap can fit neatly into your everyday life.

Kendra Adachi—self-named the "Lazy Genius"—is a proponent of the seventeen-minute nap, while I prefer twenty-five minutes (five to fall asleep, twenty to truly rest). Short rests with an alarm set—even if you don't fall asleep—allow your brain to reset without feeling groggy afterward. Whether you're a weekend marathon napper or a power napper, try incorporating a daily rest into your afternoons. Ideally, find a spot where you can turn off the light, shut the door (I used to hang a sign outside my office that said "I'm taking a mini sabbath; see you in 15 minutes" so people would know not to knock), and possibly add in a little white noise from your phone.

Preparation: Rest Kits

My artist friend taught me about the process of "gesso-ing" a canvas before painting. She wanted to have a few canvases ready for when inspiration struck, so she applied a primer called gesso ahead of time. It made me wonder about the ways in which we can apply gesso to our lives, preparing ourselves for rest and nourishment.

One of the popular fiction series when I was growing up was *The Baby-Sitters Club*. In the books, a group of entrepreneurial teens started a childcare business and shared tips, including "Kid Kits": boxes they brought along to jobs filled with activities for rainy days and bored kids. Many of us want to claim rest but don't always have the energy to come up with ideas, so we fall back on binge-watching TV or scrolling social media. What if you had your own pre-stocked Rest Kits?

If you have a typical spot you retreat to in the evenings, like the living room couch, consider putting a basket nearby filled with a favorite book, craft project, crossword, or puzzle. These are things you can easily reach for instead of falling into the familiar but not always life-giving habits of phone scrolling or binge watching. Create a list on your phone of high dopamine activities, like taking a walk, playing a favorite album, calling a friend, or baking. Having these thought out and accessible ahead of when you're feeling weary allows you to choose true rest more easily.

Awe: Seeking Spring

One late winter morning, I took my dog for a walk, and it seemed like the first time she'd ever been outside. Patches of snow were still in place, but the warming temperatures brought new discoveries. The melt uncovered several long-forgotten artifacts, and she spent a long time sniffing every inch of the yard. I, too, found myself searching for signs of new life: the crocuses peeping through the still-frozen ground, the sound of birds chirping, the spring air which filled my lungs. The winter had been far too harsh—too much death, more labor than rest, not enough connection—so I was eagerly seeking spring.

The thing about positive emotions like awe, gratitude, and delight is that we have to cultivate them. They don't always come to us organically, or when they do, we don't always notice. I recall one summer when the neighborhood children spent several hours a week playing in the yard, chasing butterflies. Their focus was such a joy to behold. Chasing butterflies and looking for signs of resurrection require a patience and hopefulness not found in many adults I know. I invite you into a resurrection scavenger hunt; perhaps you can drive through the neighborhood when a rainbow pops up to see if you can find its beginning. Or text a newly discovered poem to a friend. Spring doesn't always come like a field of wildflowers, but often one tiny bud at a time.

Retreat: Spaciousness and Space

In January 2021, after ten months of the global pandemic and a political insurrection, I texted my partner: *Let's take the kids somewhere magical this summer. A National Park or somewhere with magnificent beauty.* His response (because he entertains my impracticalities) was *YES.* Neither of us knew quite what we were signing up for, and definitely couldn't have predicted the eleven-day westward RV trip we were about to start planning. I knew even in the planning that this wasn't just about the kids. It was about my soul, and the deep spaciousness it longed for.

On this westward journey, what I was most seeking was a change of scenery. We marveled at the lands of the Shoshone, Blackfeet, and many other tribes. We visited Grand Teton, Yellowstone, and Glacier National Parks. And we encountered beauty too magnificent for words. What I noticed most was the spaciousness. Not only on the open roads through which the strong winds would ripple and rock our home on wheels. But in my entire being. I realized that leading up to the trip, I hadn't been breathing as deeply, my brain hadn't been as cleared of anxious thoughts, and my joy and gratitude hadn't come as freely as they did out in God's abundant creation.

As you begin to claim retreat, think about where you most encounter spaciousness. Sometimes you don't even need to leave home. If you're trying to find even 15 minutes set apart, seek a change in scenery: sit in a different chair or set up a small altar. Your altar might contain a candle, art, a book of poetry or prayer, and a meditation cushion or soft blanket. Having these things nearby means that you can always find a moment for retreat.

Kinship: Creation

"Go touch grass." This phrase has become a go-to in social media comment sections as a response to people who are opining on the internet. It's a not-so-soft suggestion to get off your phone and go outside, but the logic behind it is solid.

For a while in my twenties, I was a *barefooter*. That is, I walked places barefoot, ran in thin-soled barefoot shoes, and always removed my shoes before entering a church to preach or celebrate. My practice was dual parts physical (helping heal back and neck injuries) and spiritual (taking inspiration from God's words spoken to Moses at the burning bush: remove your sandals, for you are standing on holy ground). It was a healing practice for me, though others didn't always understand or support it. The most profound takeaway was that I began to notice plants and insects that I had previously overlooked. Some have spikes and we consider them dangerous to humans. But another way to tell that story is that humans are dangerous to the plants and insects.

We've often held the narrative that we humans are the stewards of God's creation, but Potawatomi botanist and author Robin Wall Kimmerer reframes the creation story: Since we are created last, everything else is our elder. This perspective shift invites us to consider what we might learn from our non-human kin. Make time today to touch the earth, let the sun hit your face, or feel the wind in your hair.

A Prayer
for Seeking Life

O Bringer of Respite and Peace,
who created the entire world
and then chose rest:
Thank you for rolling away the stone,
that we may find our burdens lightened
and joy close at hand.
May we turn our entire being
toward resurrection and new life.
May our spirit, once broken,
believe there is goodness ahead.
Lead us to claim the rest that all of Your children
so deeply need and deserve.
In weariness and hope we pray,
Amen.

PART

7

Reigniting Your Spark

When a stranger asks what I do, I have a variety of answers. I admittedly reserve "I'm a priest" for occasions when I have the time and energy to hear a confession, bear witness to people's pain with institutional religion, or offer relationship counseling. But I almost always include, "I help people find their spark." In Church world, we sometimes use the phrase *vocational discernment* to talk about the listening that goes into connecting with your purpose, but I don't think that phrase resonates with everyone. When I talk about *finding your spark*, people understand that right away, and within five minutes they usually tell me about that dream or purpose or vision they're striving toward. From taxi drivers to hair stylists, fellow clergy to people on the streets, everyone seems to long to connect with deeper meaning in their lives.

I once took a rideshare trip with a driver who stacks his shifts as a flight paramedic so that he has time to travel to the Costa Rican rainforest each month. He saves all his money and buys up areas of the rainforest, an acre at a time, in order to preserve it. His whole being came alive as he told me about his passion and life purpose.

In my encounters, I find that lots of folks I talk with have lost their spark in their job or in a relationship. Some are looking to find themselves again after retiring or becoming a parent. My first "Find Your Spark" retreat attracted retirees who were searching for meaning after being defined by their jobs for their whole career, divorcées struggling to redefine themselves and claim their worth outside of their marriage, young adults figuring out how to lead a life of purpose, and widows seeking life after death.

Everyone, regardless of age or background, was looking to discover a spark in their life. And I suspect the same is true for you, dear ones. Your gifts are many and your longing for purpose is deep. Each of you is striving to follow God's will for your life and eager to know whether your contributions can make a difference in this world.

It's not just us humans who delight in finding our spark in life. To quote early church father Irenaeus, "The glory of God is the human being fully alive." God delights in us embodying our purpose! It's no coincidence that the image of light is so often used when someone finds their purpose in scripture or literature. Connecting with your true purpose is like turning on a lamp in a dimly lit room: the light can be simultaneously surprising, disorienting, and welcome.

Each of you is equipped with extraordinary gifts which can bring more love and more light to this weary world. You have the power and resources to advocate, organize, mobilize, and create change. Making time to find and tend your spark can help you remember yourself and your faith and feel fully alive.

17

Begin Again

[S]uddenly from heaven there came a sound like the rush of a violent wind, and it filled the entire house where they were sitting. Divided tongues, as of fire, appeared among them, and a tongue rested on each of them. All of them were filled with the Holy Spirit and began to speak in other languages, as the Spirit gave them ability.

—Acts 2:2–4

I will always remember the day that my Sunday school teacher gathered us into the makeshift Sunday school room and handed a piece of paper to every child, encouraging us to draw and scribble all over it, and eventually crumple it up. She said each day you do some things that are pretty and some things that are messy. "But then," she said as she handed each of us a blank sheet of paper, "this is what God gives you every morning: a fresh piece of paper to begin again."

Never has a Sunday school lesson stuck with me like that one. Over the years, it helped me understand grace: nothing I could do could keep God from loving me and continuing to invite me into my very best self, day after day after day. On my worst days, I look forward to the promise of that blank piece of paper.

I often think of Pentecost as a chance for the disciples to begin again. Many of them didn't understand or believe

Jesus when he prepared them for his death, or if they did, they seemingly forgot what to do in the immediate aftermath of their grief. Having gone through grief myself, I can understand. I imagine the time between resurrection and ascension to be a professor-hosted study session, where Jesus says to his disciples, "Now this time, pay attention. And take notes!" Even if they (or we) didn't pick up what we needed to learn the first time, there's another chance. And on Pentecost, when the disciples become on fire with the gospel, they begin to live out their own purpose in the Reign of God.

You might be in a vocation where you go through the movements but don't feel the fire, whether that be your job, your marriage, a friendship, or some other piece of your identity. I've companioned many individuals for whom this is the case in their ministry. We often talk about what needs to change for them to connect with their spark again. In other words, is it time to leave, or—if you stay—what would it look like to make things new?

I don't ask those questions lightly. I've certainly been in relationships and in work environments that were no longer life-giving and stayed for a variety of reasons: fear, finances, faithfulness, feeling stuck, and more. If you've lost your way, left a toxic situation, or decided to stay and begin again, you're not alone. It may feel like you're starting from scratch, and perhaps you are. As in kintsugi—the Japanese art technique introduced earlier of using gold lacquer to amplify the cracks in a piece of pottery—the broken pieces of your story will still be present. But you and *you alone* get to choose how and when to display those broken pieces or share them with others.

What if your faith is the place you feel stuck or stagnant? This can be especially difficult for those of us whose professions revolve around supporting the spiritual lives of others. It is certainly not uncommon to lack the Pentecostal fire you once had.

If you've lost your faith or your fire, there's a chance to begin again. It's not too late. In the next two chapters, I'll introduce some ways to remember yourself and your spiritual practices, including making time to dream and inviting others on the journey.

Most everyone I know has had to begin again at some point or another. It may be making a move or job change, welcoming a child into your family, coming out, or adapting to life after divorce or death. Here's what I've learned from listening to the stories of those who have started over.

Change your perspective. My friend Sarah moved her family across the country for a new job. She had been living under the open skies of Lake Tahoe, where her attention was often drawn upward toward the heavens. There was so much goodness to be seen there: mountains, the lake off in the distance, snow falling. Her new landscape was so wildly different, and as she took time to grieve what she so deeply missed, she discovered something that surprised her. The land around her new home was covered by forest, and the forest floor was lined with fungi. The roots she and her family were putting down in this new and foreign place required her not to look up, but to look down. Where she once found beauty in the sky, she now finds it in the earth. Changing her perspective helped her embrace her new reality.

Show up for your healing. Beginning again may be something you never asked for or something you didn't choose lightly. Just like we all encounter the wilderness differently, your new beginning may be a big and exciting adventure or something that feels wildly terrifying. I have a friend who told me about her new beginning after several small strokes took her down a very scary and unexpected path. While she didn't desire or choose the journey, she recognized the places she had agency starting anew: it was hers to decide how to show up and support her own healing—through physical therapy, speech therapy, and so much more. Even when you weren't looking for a new beginning, I wonder how you might find healing there?

Take time to grieve. When beginning again requires leaving something behind, you will want to make extra time and space for the grief that may arise. After my divorce, my co-parent and I decided to each move back to the city where our kids had been born, as a commitment to continue parenting together and trying to reconnect with community. I prepared the kids for their move, reached out to friends in our old city so they'd feel grounded, and set up our new apartment as cozily as possible. It was a good and healing move for me, but I failed to make space for all the big emotions that come up in a transition, even when that transition is a positive one. My children and I needed space for naming fears and shedding tears.

Sometimes when you begin anew—move across the country, start a new job, begin dating after a difficult breakup—you're filled with so much hope, only to be disappointed all over again. Like turning the calendar page to January, you may think you'll leave all your sorrows and the evils of the past behind you, only to find that some of them are here, too. What might it look like to pause to mourn what has been lost and rest your heart and body for what lies ahead? Perhaps this new step can be *part* of your journey, not just a destination. There is healing ahead. Every day is a new page, a fresh chance at hope. If this one doesn't bring every hope you've been clinging to, there's always tomorrow and the next day.

Reflection Questions

Recall a story of a time when you had to begin again and
what that process looked like for you.

Discuss the role of grace in the concept of beginning again,
both spiritually and practically.

CHAPTER

18

Be Still and Know

> If we laugh and sing a little as we fight the good fight of
> freedom, it makes it all go easier. I will not allow my life's
> light to be determined by the darkness around me.
>
> —*Sojourner Truth*

On my thirty-sixth birthday, I sat in a California coffee shop just off the Pacific Ocean, sipping the most delicious chai I'd ever had and marveling at the simple beauty of the space. It was inspired space, the kind that stirred both my brain and my heart. I had been wondering how to tie together my passion and gifts of teaching, leading, creating, and gathering community. It was there, on my own birthday, that my next big dream was born. I dreamed of a place where other dreams could come to life from start to finish: an inspired space where your spark is discovered and visioning is encouraged, a space equipped with the tools and support needed to be able to tell the story of your dream, a space where creativity is cultivated and where community flourishes. In that season, I felt certain that space—*The Epiphany Space*—was a brick-and-mortar building. But with the shifts we all made during the pandemic, I was able to realize it was so much more. It was space I created digitally when I gathered weary folks for a Bring Your Own Cabin Retreat online. It was space I created in person when I led a Dream Big cohort last year and invited those gathered to share their dreams and have them illuminated in community. It's in this book, beckoning you to live into the wholeness to which God calls you.

Each year, I set aside dreaming time: solo retreats filled with silence, coffee shops with a notebook on my birthday, intentional and spontaneous conversations with dear ones, time on the water in the clear presence of God. None of my dreams would have been born if I hadn't taken the time to get quiet and listen. We all have dreams within us; they simply need a chance to be spoken, space to breathe and grow.

When we create spaces for stillness and dreaming, we also give ourselves a chance to see what might be missing in our spiritual life.

During pregnancy I learned that cravings weren't something I was supposed to ignore, but something that taught me about what I most needed. The cliché of pickles and ice cream felt unrealistic until the day I found myself buying a jar of pickles and eating them as soon as I got outside of the store. I'd never willingly eaten a pickle in my life, but my body was low on much-needed sodium and trying to tell me that. It's not just food that our body craves; I've started to listen to something I call soul cravings as well.

Soul cravings are those longings for more peace, wonder, stillness, or wholeness. When I'm companioning someone preparing for a sabbatical or creating a rule of life, I invite them to start listening to these soul cravings. A soul craving might be seeing a friend's photos of the beach and yearning to be near water. Even if it's not possible for you to go to the beach, what else might fulfill that desire? Is there a smaller body of water near you? Is your desire about having a day off or time to soak up the warmth of sunshine or read a book for pleasure? When you feel a soul craving arise, write it down and listen to what it might be calling you into.

There's an opportunity to reconnect not only with your spiritual practices but with the piece of yourself that craves those things. During a recent Lenten season, I found myself anchored in the word *warmth*. It seemed an odd word for a cold time of year and a liturgical season typically marked by self-denial. But I allowed myself to get curious and imagine what my soul was missing. I ended up finding a local spa with individual saunas, which was perfect in many ways: it allowed me to work up a sweat while my mobility was limited by a bone break and helped me face the cold mornings with a little more grace. More so, this warmth practice became ritual—time during which I meditated, immersed myself in sound bath healing or nature sounds, and reconnected with the Holy. If you feel guilty for letting your spiritual practices fall away or feel embarrassed about the soul cravings you're experiencing, offer a word of gentle compassion to yourself. The wild soul that resides within you wants to draw you closer to God. Listen.

My oldest child is someone for whom lots of things come easily. They practically came out of the womb speaking and have engaged adults in conversation since their toddler years; they readily make new friends and have a creative mind that crafts without needing a pattern. So when they asked to play cello in fifth grade, I was thrilled. They were too, until it came time to lug the large instrument back and forth to school every Monday. My now-teenager reflected back on that experience and shared that they were a bit defeated because they never got good at the cello. I chuckled a bit and said, "Did you ever even practice?" My kid laughed and sheepishly admitted no.

We use the word *practice* for rhythms in our life that we want to reinforce, like spiritual practices and self-care practices. From time to time, I forget that those things actually require my attention and effort. They are called a *practice* after all. If I were in a play and had play practice, I would need to show up to most—if not all—scheduled rehearsals. How often do you show up for your own practices?

I have a dear friend who makes time for journaling, meditation, and movement each morning. I'm in awe of her practice, but it never feels possible for me, so sometimes I'm tempted to throw in the towel before I've even tried. In those moments, I try to remember that a little bit is more than nothing. When I used to run regularly, there were plenty of mornings when I didn't feel like I could muster the energy, but I'd make a deal with myself: go out for a half-mile warmup, check in with myself, and then give myself permission to go home, if needed. More often than not, I would press myself onward by stretching just a bit further, and then a bit more beyond that, and I'd feel grateful afterward. On the days when I only had that half mile in me, that was okay too. When you don't have the energy to engage in a spiritual practice, I wonder if you could set aside just five minutes for being still.

Sometimes I encounter the Holy when I get really still, and sometimes it happens when I'm moving throughout the world. Like a writer who keeps a notebook on their person at all times in case their muse appears or inspiration strikes, we can help prepare ourselves to receive these interactions. Experts in dream analysis say the best way to remember your dreams is to put paper and pen on your bedside table in order to capture fleeting images and thoughts upon waking. If we want to capture our waking dreams, we must be intentional and provide ourselves with the proper tools for creating and cultivating space for dreaming.

One morning, I awoke early and felt something stirring in my soul. It was a new moon that morning, so the predawn sky was dim. I leaned into the beautiful, quiet darkness and listened carefully. I knew it was about my vocational path, but the details were unclear. So I committed to spend the next six months paying attention. To what, I wasn't yet sure, but I knew my spark needed tending. I marked my calendar, and asked my spiritual director and some beloveds to companion me. Six months later, I opened a notebook and let the Holy Spirit flow through me. My partner looked over at me that day and commented on the brightness of my eyes. I told him it was the brightness that comes when my spirit is on fire. Even if your intention is simply to pay attention, that's enough.

You cannot share with others that which you yourself do not have, so take time to tend your fire.

Reflection Questions

How do you find stillness in your life, and what does it bring to your spiritual practice?

Share an experience where listening to your "soul cravings" led to a deeper understanding or a meaningful change.

Reflect on the importance of dreaming and creating space for your dreams to grow. How do you set aside time to cultivate your dreams?

19

Setting Fires

Someday, after we have mastered the winds, the waves and gravity, we shall harness for God energies of love. Then for the second time in the history of the world we will have discovered fire.

—*Teilhard de Chardin*

I'm really good at *starting* fires. One summer, I took a couple of days of retreat at a cabin in the woods. There was no Wi-Fi or cell signal, so it was perfect for disconnecting and imagining myself as an explorer of the great outdoors. The first evening, I tried to start a fire in the fire pit. I used all my outdoorsy knowledge and recalled the advice of my partner, the Eagle Scout, starting with the smallest kindling and working my way up toward bigger logs, all built conically.

Then I set about tending my fire. I kept a close eye on it, ready to respond to whatever it showed me it needed. I poked and prodded, set more kindling aflame, and re-adjusted the wood. The effect was rather underwhelming. The initial flare was replaced mostly by smoke on the less-than-dry sticks.

I had been trying really hard to take care of my Spark in that season, the sense of deep meaning and purpose that resides within each of us. I didn't always have the right tools. Sometimes the conditions weren't ideal, and all I had to work with was damp wood.

Tending your Spark is immensely more difficult than setting a fire. You may feel like you're stalled or failing. Maybe you can't even find your Spark to begin with. Perhaps you're too exhausted to give it the attention it needs. And you may wonder if you'll ever be able to see your dream come to life.

It doesn't need to be a solo act. In fact, reconnecting with your spirit and your purpose is something you can and sometimes must do in relationship with others. When we read the story of the first Pentecost, with people speaking in multiple languages, I often hear a focus on what a miracle it was that people were able to speak in tongues. Years ago, I heard a Pentecost sermon about how it's not just a miracle of the tongue, but a miracle of the ear. After all, what good is a bunch of people speaking in new languages if there's no one there to listen and interpret? When the Holy Spirit shows up, we need a companion to speak while we listen or listen while we speak.

I call this act co-dreaming. I have several people in my life who are my co-dreamers. My friend Jerusalem and I spend long sessions in co-dreaming. Whether we're scheming up a joint venture or helping the other through a stuck place, we love setting up intentional time to support each other's wildest dreams. These sessions aren't just about cheering each other on, but listening to the fear, scarcity, and comparison, and helping to be a voice of truth and empathy. My greatest co-dreamer is my partner, and our co-dreaming usually involves demoing a room in our house and several trips to the hardware store. When either of us sees a gleam

of the eye and hears, "What if we . . . ?" we should probably walk away quickly.

By dreaming with others, I hear my own desires and
gifts reflected back to me. I gain new perspective. I'm given
permission to dream even more wildly. And I get to offer
the same to others.

I've heard it said that we need to surround ourselves with
people who will sing the song of our hearts back to us
when we forget the words. Even so, again and again I
encounter folks who deeply desire meaningful community and don't know how to access it. This is what I've
experienced and witnessed when it comes to cultivating
community.

Find a fourth space. In the concept of the third place,
home and work are our first two primary spaces. The idea
is that we need a third place where we can find belonging.
Sometimes this is a coffee shop or coworking space; often
it's a faith community. If you work in the church, it can't
fully be your third space. Where else can you find meaning,
connection, and community?

Don't be the expert. We're often in positions where we
need to be the expert in the room. Since ministry would
require him to be skilled at most things, one of my seminary classmates had a mentor who suggested that he pick
up a hobby he wasn't any good at. So before we graduated,
my friend took up skateboarding. It seemed a bit ridiculous
to watch him learn this skill in adulthood, but the inevita-
ble falls were a great lesson in taking himself less seriously.
It's important to put ourselves in places where we don't
know the answers or where we're trying something completely outside of our comfort zone, something completely

new. What do those experiences look like? What do they teach us?

Create the thing you need. I'm admittedly brazen when it comes to forming friendships. My friends Katie and Liz are dear friends because—despite only meeting in person once before—I called and asked if I could travel to their cities and stay with them. When I meet a person who has something I desire in a friend, I simply ask if they want to be my friend. I risk being perceived as awkward, but the reward is often a deep and abiding relationship. If you're seeking community or wanting to make a friend, start a book club or invite someone to coffee. How might you cultivate community?

Share your story. Remember the chapter on vulnerability and trust? Modeling vulnerability encourages others to do the same. If you share your dreams or let your spark burn bright, others will know they have space to do the same. Your story matters and could spark someone else to find belonging, feel love, or remember their purpose. The entire story of Pentecost is about spreading the good news throughout the land. What's your good news to share?

Call on the Holy Spirit. We are promised that whenever two or three are gathered, God will be in our midst. Whether you're stuck or seeking new life, the Holy Spirit is your helper. The Holy Spirit can be unpredictable and appear like a peaceful dove or like the rush of a violent wind. If you close yourself off from the Holy Spirit, you close yourself off from an invitation into more. Remember, you don't have to tend your spark all alone.

Reflection Questions

Reflect on your process of setting and tending to your own spark. What challenges and successes have you encountered?

How can co-dreaming with others enhance your ability to connect with your purpose and passions?

In what ways do you cultivate community in your own life?

Part 7
SPARK Practice

nurture my **S**oma
engage in **P**reparation
make space for **A**we
claim **R**etreat
ground myself in **K**inship

Soma: Grounding

Feet flat on the floor, hands resting on knees in a posture of receptivity (palms up) or rootedness (palms down). I often begin retreats with this invitation for participants to ground themselves. After breaks, I draw us back together with the same exercise of grounding, and by the second or third time I do this, people toss whatever is on their laps to the floor and uncross their limbs so quickly you'd think there was a fire. I take this as a sign that they've tapped into something deeply resonant in the practice of grounding and they can't wait to experience it again.

Grounding isn't only for times when we're feeling anxious. In a creative season, I feel as if the Holy Spirit courses through me, filling me with ideas and energy and a clear sense of God's will for me. It's a wonderful feeling, and yet . . . the Holy Spirit isn't always a gentle dove. She's also depicted as a violent wind, and I have to be careful to not get blown away. Staying grounded in generative times is difficult because the realm of creative energy can be hard to turn off. It resides very closely with sleeplessness and anxiety; creative energy keeps our wheels turning.

You can ground yourself through meditation, eating nourishing foods, focusing on being present to your beloveds, and striving to tend to your body through sleep and movement. You might also notice when your body needs to push or pull. When you're feeling angry or fearful, try an activity that allows you to push against something, like pressing your palms against your knees or a wall. This somatic exercise can allow your body to release big emotions.

Preparation: Examen

Sometimes what we need most is to surface for air. I call this "reflect and reset," courtesy of my friend Jenn Giles Kemper (creator of *Sacred Ordinary Days*). This weekly practice of Reflect and Reset is inspired by the Ignatian spiritual practice of the Daily Examen: becoming aware of God's presence, reviewing your day with gratitude, asking for guidance, and looking ahead to tomorrow. I suggest using a framework that you can check in on regularly. You can easily use the SPARK spokes for this exercise (e.g., How have I been nurturing my soma? In what areas of my life do I want to focus on preparation? Where have I witnessed awe this week? What does claiming retreat look like for me in the next season? In what ways have I engaged in kinship?).

Reflect on how these things have gone well or fallen short in the past week or season, and reset by naming intentions in these categories for the week or season to come. Here are a few guiding questions: Where did God/goodness/light show up today? Where did you struggle to see

God/goodness/light? As you look ahead to tomorrow, what excites you? What fills you with fear or hesitation?

Awe: Music

At Red Rocks Amphitheatre, a stunning venue (some might call it a cathedral), I had one of the most powerful musical experiences of my life. We were there to see the incredibly talented bluegrass musician Billy Strings. For the hours that Billy and his band were on stage, it seemed as if every one of the 9500 people in the audience were on their feet. What's more, they were all moving to the music. Several times, I caught myself turning in a full circle to witness a community of strangers pulsing to a shared vibration. It was a deeply spiritual experience, as if we were all engaged in the same prayer.

My partner says that music is a communal act of allowing others to pray for you when you don't have the words. Whether you prefer live music or quietly listening at home, music has a way of invoking and capturing awe. Find music you like, ask for recommendations from others, and share what you love.

Retreat: Silence

No matter how many podcasts I have downloaded, when I get in my car and head out on a road trip, I often find myself driving for an hour or more in complete silence. It's never intentional, but what my soul craves.

Silence isn't for everyone, but our lives are often filled with too much noise. What would an adaptation look like for you? Instead of silent meditation, try meditating while moving through nature. Or playing soft instrumental music to open space within you but not consume your thoughts.

You might even try a meal with others where you sit in silence and focus on communicating in other ways. Find ways to incorporate more quiet into your day-to-day life.

Kinship: Reciprocity

In our baptismal covenant, we vow to "respect the dignity of every (human) being."

Robin Wall Kimmerer shares an experience of gathering leeks from the land under the Sugar Maples and noticing that they were all crowded together in her gathering basket. She knew that she had the ability to notice their needs and ask how they would best thrive, and named this process of noticing and responding *reciprocity*.

We are invited to live in reciprocity with one another, continually noticing and asking what the other needs and sharing our own needs in response.

This includes sharing your light and inviting others to share theirs. In *Atlas of the Heart*, Brené Brown talks about how she and her husband always taught their kids that "good friends aren't afraid of your light. They never blow out your flame and you don't blow out theirs." Who in your life can be a light-bearer? Who will cup your flame when it's about to blow out?

A Prayer
for Tending Our Fire

O Radiant Fire,
glowing so brightly we must shield our eyes;
O Holy Spirit,
quiet as a dove and forceful as a wind:
do not let us be unmoved.
Light a fire within us
that burns so deeply we cannot ignore.
Grant us strength to begin again
and courage to speak our wildest dreams.
Shield us from the hubris of needing to be the expert
and give us the eyes and heart of a novice,
until Your dazzling presence comes down again,
Amen.

PART

8

Integrating Creativity and Sustainability

I once set out to knit a liturgical year wrap. It was a project with 365 rows, each row corresponding to the liturgical color of the season. As I picked out my colors—a deep blue for Advent, a regal purple for Lent, a special gold for Easter, and so on, I found myself pausing on the green for Ordinary Time. Instead of buying one green yarn to knit a majority of the year, I opted for multiple shades of green to keep me interested in the project and to represent the shifts that happen even in Ordinary Time. (Did I finish the wrap? Dear reader, I did not. I'm still somewhere in Lent.)

Ordinary Time sometimes seems like the space in between more interesting seasons, but—according to the children's formation program Godly Play—it is the Great Green Growing season. If you've made it to this point in the book, you've put a lot of heart into reflecting on burnout and implementing life-giving practices for mitigating and keeping it at bay. As with any big life change, we have a surge of energy at first; it's the maintenance phase, or the keeping up with it, that sometimes feels monotonous. In these final chapters, I'll invite you to connect with your creativity—an ever-changing and sustaining piece of your identity—as well as your childlike wonder. Finally, I'll ask you to name and reinforce the things in your life that feel most nourishing.

As Dory says while swimming the expansive ocean in *Finding Nemo*: "Just keep swimming."

Just Keep Swimming

The fullness of joy is to behold God in everything. God is the ground, the substance, the teaching, the teacher, the purpose, and the reward for which every soul labors.

—*Julian of Norwich*

A s I began my transition from traditional parish ministry to entrepreneurial creative ministry, I kept finding myself in conversations with sibling faith leaders who were also creatives: Hillary, a theologian and writer rethinking the way we gather in community; Eric, who writes a poem every single day; Roger, an incredible photographer and artist; Meg, a skilled storyteller. I realized that there are so many creatives longing to lean even further into their creativity. Many of the burnt-out clergy and ministry professionals I have talked to dream—at least occasionally—of another path outside of parish ministry. And often that path involves feeding their creativity.

Every time I talk with a group about creativity, a handful of folks say, "I don't have a creative bone in my body." If that's you, here's the good news: we're all creatives! During one retreat, I asked participants to name the ways they were creative. After clearing out the more obvious ones—knitting, painting, writing, singing—people started to think outside the box. "I'm really good at rearranging furniture in a room," one person said. Others followed: "I'm good at creating spreadsheets," "I like to organize and plan events," "I love pairing different prints and patterns together," "I can put together IKEA furniture without the instructions." Being creative doesn't have to mean that you know what to do with a blank canvas. Being creative is about doing the things which *you* can do and doing them well.

We've explored the idea of comparison many times throughout this book. Comparison might be the thing that makes you hesitant to embrace creativity. While you might feel like being creative subjects you to comparison, it actually does the opposite. Creativity is an *antidote* for comparison because your creation is an expression of your individuality. Even if you were to attend a painting class where everyone was given the same mountainscape, you would choose your colors, decide how tall your peaks would be, and make your own unique piece of art. A sweater I knit from a pattern will look different from another sweater made using the same exact pattern. Our creativity is like our fingerprint: no one else can copy it.

Comparison is rooted in the Latin "match with," and the early French understanding would have been "regard or treat as equal." The stuff that activates our shame voices most isn't completely different from what we're doing; it's often similar in some way. It's close enough for us to feel like we've fallen short. I'm unlikely to compare my athletic skills to my incredibly tall and coordinated godson, but I might peer over at a woman close to my age easily getting into crow position in a yoga class. Our great act of resistance to those voices can be to create something: cook a meal, rearrange a room, color, draw, mold, organize a spreadsheet, sing, dance, plan an event, write, work with your hands. The thing you create will be yours, not subject to the opinions of others.

All I ask is that you strive to appreciate it as an offering of *imago dei* (the image of God), not poking and prodding and wondering how it could be better or different or more like someone else's creation.

While one path to finding your spark might be leaving your current position to pursue your creative dreams, another path might be incorporating your creativity into your current vocation or as a hobby in your life. It's up to you to decide whether you want to use your creative gifts in a paid setting. It's tempting for others to want to monetize anything we love—*oh wow, you make beautiful earrings! you should sell them!*—so you'll need to decide whether your creativity is something you want to share with others or produce. It isn't necessary to *productivize* everything we do. Here are some benefits to simply creating for yourself:

It doesn't have to be perfect. Perfectionism acts as a false guard against shame, because we think that if we're always still working on it, we know it isn't perfect and thus others can't hurt us with their criticism. As a knitter, there are a couple of options I have when I notice I made a mistake several rows earlier: I can "frog" it, which means ripping out the rows all the way back to the mistake and starting again. I can also assess my mistake and ask myself whether it's going to bother me or simply add character to the garment. Neither option is right or wrong, but I'm the only one who gets to decide which option is best for me. In a world in which people can nitpick about a misplaced comma in the bulletin, it's healthy and healing to have spaces where you can create just for you.

It doesn't even have to be complete. Creativity doesn't always have to end in a finished project. There can be something satisfying about trying out new craft tools or art supplies without an idea in mind. If your leadership role means you have to plan ahead for all of the possible outcomes or feel responsible for the well-being of your family and church members, it can be freeing to have an outlet where everything isn't critical. Maybe creating without a plan feels challenging to you. You can start small by giving yourself space each week for non-professional writing or taking time with a few colored pencils and a piece of paper. You're not trying to win any awards here; you're simply trying to reconnect with your soul.

During the pandemic, my partner and I bought a house that needed several updates. With less travel in our lives and more time on our hands, we channeled our creative energy into home renovations. We loved many things about these types of projects. First, they were completely unrelated to our work skill set. We got to revel in being new learners at something again—thanks, YouTube!—and feed our inquisitiveness. We also got to focus on what was right in front of us. I find that most creative projects require my full attention, making it nearly impossible to fall into the trap of mindlessly scrolling my phone. Finally, even though I said creative projects don't have to be complete, there can also be great satisfaction and joy in completing something.

Creativity is generative. Whether you choose to incorporate your creativity into your work or keep it as a side hobby, thinking and acting creatively will spill over into all aspects of your life. Conversely, not being able to exercise your creative muscles will make it more difficult to come up with creative solutions to problems or generate new ideas. I once had a creative project of mine put on hold, and I stopped dreaming for a couple of years. My self-doubt was high and my trust in others to receive and hold my creativity was low, so I subconsciously closed myself off to coming up with anything new. Nurturing your creativity can have a deep impact on all aspects of your life.

Reflection Questions

Recall a time when you felt comparison hindered your creativity. How did you overcome it?

Reflect on the importance of creating for oneself versus for others. How can this affect your enjoyment and the outcomes of your creative pursuits?

CHAPTER

21

Be as a Child

Then the prophet Miriam . . . took a tambourine in her hand,
and all the women went out after her with tambourines and
with dancing.

—Exodus 15:20

Have you ever had a moment—or a season—when
you doubted your purpose in life? A time when you
wondered if your dreams were worth it or whether
it might be better to simply walk away?

One Sunday during my ordination process, I sat down in
a church I considered my spiritual home. I showed up reluc-
tantly that day. My faith had been shaken a few days earlier
when the committee responsible for walking alongside me
as I discerned a call to the priesthood had let me down. Or
so it felt at the time. They said, "We hear your call, Callie,
but we're not ready to endorse you."

Those words came as such a blow to me that I ques-
tioned my entire call and whether I wanted to continue in
the discernment process. Over the days following their decision, I wrestled with God: first writing an angry and uncen-
sored letter to/*at* God, then sitting in the pit—much as I
imagined Job having done—while I listened to God's empathy and willingness to sit with me, and finally listening to

God's words that Sunday morning when I sat in the congregation at my beloved church.

It was then, in my self-doubt and anger and hurt, that I heard these words from the prophet Jeremiah (1:4–8):

> Now the word of the Lord came to me saying, "Before I formed you in the womb I knew you, and before you were born I consecrated you; I appointed you a prophet to the nations." Then I said, "Ah, Lord God! Truly I do not know how to speak, for I am only a [child]." But the Lord said to me, "Do not say, 'I am only a [child]; for you shall go to all to whom I send you, and you shall speak whatever I command you. Do not be afraid of them, for I am with you to deliver you, says the Lord."

In that moment, I heard this not as a dialogue between God and Jeremiah, but as words spoken into my own heart. I heard God's words throughout my body: "You are called, Callie. Truth-teller. Healer. Child. Priest. You are called."

When you are filled with self-doubt, know that God meets you there. God knit you together in your mother's womb and has called you to live into your wholeness since before you were born.

Becoming as a child doesn't mean being ignorant or unknowing. It doesn't mean being unaware of the hardships and tragedies this world holds. It means tapping into the child that still abides within each of us and asking them what they see. My children are my greatest teachers in so many things. Their resilience, joy, and wonder have guided me in many hard seasons. We are no strangers to the living room dance party, that act of reckless abandon that can change the tenor of a rough morning. When I'm moving too quickly, they slow me with a question. When the pitch of my voice goes up, they ask whether I need a deep breath. When I feel heartbroken by the news of the world, they offer me a tender hug.

When I hear the story of the Parting of the Red Sea, my attention is always drawn to Miriam and her tambourine: a moment of childlike levity and joy in an episode of significant drama. I'll admit that my adult self isn't always readily available to engage in playfulness. Sometimes I'll respond to a silly kid with a stern voice, then wonder what harm their silliness was causing. In addition to the non-doing time I introduced earlier, mindful play is a tool for moving past a state of overwhelm.

Mindful play has no set outcome or goal. There's no competition, no comparison. The point of mindful play is to be present. Children have a much greater capacity for this than adults. You might choose to go on a bike ride, but not clock your time or mileage, or to throw a frisbee in your backyard. Mindful play can be anything that allows you to be present in the moment and tap into liberated joy.

When I was growing up, there was a popular poster that many educators displayed in their classrooms: "All I really need to know, I learned in kindergarten." Originally penned as a book by minister Robert Fulghum, the tips included things like share everything, play fair, don't hit people, and take a nap every afternoon. The children in our communities can remind us of so many fundamental aspects of engaging with the world:

Be attuned to your present needs. When you're young, you expect to be fed when you're hungry, and you take a nap whenever your eyes get heavy. As adults, we make it much more complicated, but it doesn't need to be. If we can reconnect with our present needs and make sure to attend to them, we'll all be healthier.

Keep your sense of wonder and hold onto your imagination. Like a kid waiting for Christmas morning, there's still magic to be found in this world. Can you let yourself experience a surge of hope? Whether it's watching a plant shoot grow or gazing at a bird outside your window, the world holds so much beauty. Imagine the feeling of falling in love; it's possible to have that again.

It's okay to need the support of others. I'm not sure at what point in the development of our brains that a switch flips and says we need to figure everything out on our own. We were created as communal creatures, and each possesses gifts that differ from one another. So it would make sense that we still need to draw on each other's support.

Seek lower ground. When my kids were toddlers, they would throw themselves onto the floor when everything got to be too much. I called it "seeking lower ground." I imagine there's something deeply biological about flattening yourself against the only stable point in the room. All your big feelings are valid. How do you make space for them?

Joy is never inappropriate. After my beloved parent died, we shared many tears. But my kids also wanted to play LEGO and tell knock-knock jokes. There were times when we laughed till we had to catch our breath. Even in the midst of grief, burnout, or tragedy, joy has a place.

Be as a child, in all the wonderful ways. Give yourself what the child within you always longed for. Allow yourself to be held and nurtured and loved.

Reflection Questions

What does it mean to you to "become as a child" in the context of faith and life?

How can embracing playfulness and childlike qualities contribute to your spiritual and emotional health?

CHAPTER

22

Give Us This Bread Always

Then Jesus said to [his disciples], "Very truly, I tell you, it was not Moses who gave you the bread from heaven, but it is my Father who gives you the true bread from heaven. For the bread of God is that which comes down from heaven and gives life to the world." They said to him, "Sir, give us this bread always."

—*John 6:32–24*

W hen my children were young, I used to have a trailer that attached to my bike. I can clearly remember a Saturday morning bike ride through a tree-canopied trail with them in tow. I felt pure and deep joy in my heart and said to myself, "Give us this bread always." When I think of the joy and satisfaction the Israelites felt after discovering manna one morning in the desert, and the subsequent assurance Jesus' disciples felt after hearing that same story, I resonate with their feeling of deep soul-level satisfaction.

As we near the end of our journey together, I invite you to reflect on the moments in your life that sustain you the most. I've shared my personal practice of using the word *return* in a wilderness season to notice when I was feeling most myself. When I do feel full of life, gratitude, or joy, I try to pause. The moments aren't always profound, but usually an everyday memory. Many times, it's been something as simple as cooking a nourishing meal, taking a moment to soak up the sun and rest in the backyard hammock, or laughing myself silly with my beloveds.

The act of returning can be a turning away or a turning toward. When I was first ordained, I didn't feel particularly drawn to the practice of celebrating the Eucharist at an East-facing altar, wherein the priest turns away from the congregation to say the blessing over the communion table. Many churches have pulled the altar away from the wall so that it stands between the clergy and the people, both looking on the Eucharistic meal together. But then I served a church with an East-facing altar and was given an image not of turning away from the people, but joining them in all turning toward God together. I found that this positioning also allowed me to enter more fully into prayer, which is not always easy when you're leading.

Several summers ago, when my family traveled westward to Yellowstone and Glacier National Parks, our first stop was the Chapel of the Transfiguration in Grand Teton National Park. As I stepped inside, I was immediately drawn toward the altar facing the rear wall of the church and the window above it, which looked out over the mountains. Even though I'd never been there before, I was returning. I respectfully moved the altar rail aside and took my place at the table, standing in the traditional prayer posture for giving thanks over the bread and the wine. I turned, not away from those gathered there in prayer, but toward. Toward abundance, toward beauty, toward the Holy.

Whether you're still immersed in weariness or finding yourself embracing wholeheartedness, know that you are called to spaces of sustaining goodness and wonder. Cling tight to the moments when you feel yourself and recognize the Holy in your midst.

In 2021, shortly after I was introduced to the term "languishing"—that mental state of not-quite-ill-not-quite-well, characterized by brain fog, lack of motivation, and a general feeling of blah—I learned about flourishing, the opposite of languishing. Many of the tips for moving toward flourishing were based on Martin Seligman's PERMA Theory of renewed life—**P**ositive Emotion, **E**ngagement, **R**elationships, **M**eaning, and **A**ccomplishment—as well as the research completed by Tyler VanderWeele and Harvard's Human Flourishing Program. These researchers have found what many of us already know, but don't always stop to consider: Having community, purpose, and a sense of achievement helps us feel more alive.

As I read through their various antidotes to languishing, I found the following suggestions: celebrate small things by naming moments of awe, develop a weekly gratitude practice, complete five kind acts, connect with a community, find your purpose, and try something new. I realized that those things could be found within the context of a faith community. Awe, gratitude, kindness, and purpose are core tenets of many religious bodies. In several of our traditions, we share a symbolic or literal meal each and every time we gather. The source of burnout for many of us—serving a faith community—might also be the key to wholeness. How do we draw on the sustaining practices found there and allow them to fill us up, while keeping ourselves from being depleted? It may mean that the community you serve is different from the community that serves you.

Throughout this book, I've offered you tools for cultivating community, tapping into your creativity, finding your spark, setting boundaries, avoiding comparison, and more. I wholeheartedly wish I could offer you assurance that reading this book and engaging these tools will prevent burnout. It's likely that you will find yourself on the edge of burnout again. Next time, I invite you to remember this whole set of new tools you've acquired. You have come so far, dear ones.

Having made this journey, I invite you to turn around and look with fresh eyes upon how far you've traveled. Perhaps you can see more clearly now what lies ahead. I wonder if what you need most is available to you in your vocation(s). What is sustaining you? What needs to change?

In the long growing season, we cannot simply rest in the transformation that has taken place. We must continue to choose that which is life-giving. With plenty of naps and snacks along the way, we must continue onward toward the wholeness into which God calls each and every one of us.

Reflection Questions

Reflect on the moments or practices in your life that sustain you the most. How can you incorporate more of these into your daily routine?

Think about the concept of "returning" in your life. How does coming back to familiar spiritual or joyful experiences help you in times of stress or weariness?

Part 8
SPARK Practice

nurture my **S**oma
engage in **P**reparation
make space for **A**we
claim **R**etreat
ground myself in **K**inship

Soma: Heart Check-In

"How is your heart today?" I begin all of my companioning sessions with this question, inviting deeper reflection than a simple "How are you?" We typically answer that with "fine" or "busy," something superficial enough to keep from going too deep or getting pulled into a conversation our busy selves don't have time for. Islamic scholar Omid Safi says that, in Muslim cultures, it is common to ask, "How is your haal?" It roughly translates as, "How is your heart doing at this very moment, at this breath?"

A longtime client once said, "I always look forward to this part, so I can find out how my heart is." I laughed, because of course we can always check in with ourselves, but we're much more likely to do so when invited by another person. Like the body scan, a heart check-in can make you aware of where your soul is soaring or weary, where your body is holding stress or joy. It doesn't matter how your heart was yesterday or how it will be tomorrow. Take a moment to check in with yourself.

Preparation: Stacking

Beginning new life-giving practices can be difficult. There are only so many hours in a day, and when you try to do a life overhaul (changing several habits at once), you can set yourself up for overwhelm. Instead, I love the idea of stacking new practices with already established practices. I once had a twelve-minute commute to the gym, which was the perfect length of time to listen to the daily *Pray as You Go* podcast. If you already make coffee every morning, you might add a five-minute life-giving practice while your coffee is brewing, like emptying the dishwasher, stepping outside to soak up your morning sunshine, or listening to a short meditation.

When you establish and meet small goals for yourself, you feel a sense of accomplishment, energizing you and decreasing your stress level. Find easy ways to incorporate new practices into your life.

Awe: Creation and Creativity

I sometimes fall into the fallacy that I have complete autonomy over my creativity. In reality, it ebbs and flows in ways I can't always predict. I once was in a season when I wasn't feeling myself, and everything felt a bit muted. When I sat down to write, the words I had envisioned seemed to fall flat on the page; my creative well had run dry. Even when I had the ideas, my energy was low.

I took myself on retreat with very few intentions: make nourishing meals, read for fun, get out on the water. One morning, I stepped onto a paddle board for the first time and encountered the fullness of God's creation—in all its splendor and radiance—in a new way. I inhaled deeply, wanting to breathe in the stillness and be sustained by the beauty, and exhaled, "Oh my God." The words escaped my lips as a prayer, with utmost reverence. I had been seeking Her, and there She was. At that moment, I was reminded that when the spark within me is dim, I need to seek the Spark outside of myself.

I find the creation Spark most clearly in the elements: the glass surface of the morning lake, the first flurries of the year that seem to silence all else, the fiery sunsets that make me want to proclaim God's goodness to strangers, the autumn leaves as they prepare to fall.

Creation often inspires our creativity, if we take the time to seek it out. When you find yourself struggling to speak a message of hope in a weary world, struggling to find your spark, or struggling to regain your sense of self after a long season in the wilderness, perhaps you can let the Holy guide you back home. Make time to glimpse God's unmistakable presence all around and remember the fullness of who you are.

Retreat: Soul-Tending

The phrase *self-care* has become a catchall for everything from mental therapy to retail therapy. Whether you're engaging in journaling, binge-watching, a pedicure, or drawing a bath, all of these might be considered self-care. I prefer the phrase *soul-tending*.

What is it that your soul so deeply longs for? Your soul needs tending, my dear ones. Whether it's an epic road trip or ten minutes to yourself in a locked room, it's okay to claim spaciousness. Your whole being will thank you.

If I could write you a prescription for a multiple-day retreat, I would do it right now. I'm often talking with folks who haven't had a retreat in years, if ever. *Since before my kids were born. When I was preparing for my ordination. I scheduled one but had to cancel it.*

My instruction to the people I companion is to build a retreat on-ramp. I ask:

- What can you plan by the end of this week that offers you retreat? Perhaps it's a half-hour option.
- What about by the end of this month? Can you plan time for a half day?
- And by the end of the year, what would it look like to take an overnight or more?

How can you make time to take time, setting aside even five minutes a day to nourish your spirit?

Kinship: Showing Up

I don't always want to show up. I don't always want to bring my full and authentic self to every encounter and relationship in my life. I once attended a sacred singing workshop. When we began, we were asked to share something from our hearts. I—the person who literally teaches vulnerability and wholeheartedness—sat there in the circle with my arms crossed and my lips tight. I'd been emotionally vulnerable all week, and I didn't want to show up any more.

I know my openness resonates with people, because they tell me so and because I myself am drawn toward people who model vulnerability, but sometimes I don't want to put in the work. I see this in my relationships and my parenting, too. Some days, I want to shut out everyone and everything. I scroll through my phone while spending time with my kids, or I avoid speaking up for what I need in a friendship. Then I wonder why things start deteriorating. I haven't shown up, and yet I still expect things to keep running as usual.

Belonging to one another means to show up again and again. Some days it will be easy, and some days it will be the very last thing we want to do. But showing up is the way we can stay grounded in our true selves and reclaim a little bit of power in a time of so much powerlessness. Let us journey onward together.

A Prayer
for Returning

O God of Growth,
Thank you for creating all things
and calling us into continual co-creating.
When the season feels long
and the journey feels never-ending,
invite us to turn again toward You,
toward one another,
and toward ourselves.
May we be as children
longing for playful joy.
May we offer our gifts
to this weary world.
May we persevere through it all.
Give us this bread always,
Amen.

A Blessing for the Way

How far we've come. Together, we have traveled from Advent through Ordinary Time, from peering into the tomb to seeking signs of life, from weary to wholehearted.

While writing this book, there were many times I thought of turning back. While writing this book, I companioned a beloved through their own burnout. While writing this book, I gave so much that I had to remember not to become burnt-out myself.

I also heard of your brokenness and deep wounds, and became increasingly convicted that a resource on burnout (and, if I'm honest, the need for many other resources in addition to my own) is what our weary world needs. We all need healing and rest. As I culled the research and created the SPARK Practice, I began implementing it in my own life. I began noticing the ways in which it was already innate within me, and the ways in which leaning into it led me toward flourishing.

Dear ones, as we wrap up this part of our shared journey together, I want to leave you with a blessing:

May you know that your soma is holy, and that it longs to be nourished.

May you have the wisdom to discern when it is time to prepare, and when it is time to rest in the preparations you have made.

May you be overcome with awe and always welcome it in.

May you claim times of retreat and find your soul restored.

May you ground yourself in kinship, and remember that you are never alone.

May you always return to your belovedness, the knowledge that you are made in God's own image, and that in you, God is well pleased.

In the name of the God who creates us, redeems us, and tends our Spark:

Amen.

Gratitudes

As I look over this love letter I've penned for all who are weary, I can't help but make space for awe and ground myself in kinship. These words were living within me, but it took a whole community and a persistent presence of the Holy to draw them onto the page.

I am immensely grateful to:

My family. They endured "just one more" writing task and cheered me on every step of the way. E, you asked such thoughtful questions at every point in the proposal and writing process. L, thanks for thinking I'm already famous. Jeremy patiently read every single word. Thank you for encouraging my dreams and entertaining my impracticalities. (I can't wait to plan our next adventure!)

Momma, you've always told me to listen to my heart. Dave, you always believed in me and would surely be the first in line to have your copy signed.

My editor Eve Strillacci. I recalled your sustaining words whenever I started to lose my way: *When you share your hard-learned lessons with others, you tie them to a happier future where God's abundance is more easily felt.*

My editor Justin Hoffman. You were handed the baton after the first leg; thank you for jumping in and helping me cross the finish line.

My pit crew, especially Joellynn and Allison. You make me wholehearted.

Jo Nygard Owens, thank you for calmly talking me through many stuck points.

My beloved friends, who reminded me of my strength and checked in on my heart: Hillary, Liz, Meredith, Michael,

Heidi, Jerusalem, Sarah, Traci, Sarah, Tina, Nikky, Patrick, Eric, Kaitlin, Kate. You carried me.

My magical community at The Writing Table and my writing coach, Eileen Campbell-Reed. You reminded me I'm not alone.

For inspired spaces where pieces of this book fell into place: Taqueria Amor, Lake Erie, Kirkridge Retreat Center, and Puerto Morelos.

Anyone who ever told me I should write a book. Each person who responded to my Wholehearted Wisdom writings over the years. Every church community I have ever served. You made space for the Holy Spirit.

Everyone who allowed me to share their stories, especially Melissa. And each weary and wholehearted soul I've companioned on your journey. Thank you for showing up vulnerably.

You. Thank you for opening your heart and allowing me to remind you that you are beloved and that you are never alone.